Colonial Architecture

D1614040

Old Swedes (Holy Trinity) Church, Wilmington,
from a painting by Stanley M. Arthurs

Colonial Architecture
Early Examples from the First State

George Fletcher Bennett

with Introduction and Text by Joseph L. Copeland

4880 Lower Valley Road, Atglen, PA 19310 USA

Other Schiffer Books on Related Subjects

Mississippi Valley Architecture: Houses of the Lower Mississippi Valley, Stanley Schuler
Early Domestic Architecture of Pennsylvania, Eleanor Raymond
Survey of Chester County, Pennsylvania, Architecture: Margaret B. Schiffer
Shaker Architecture: Herbert Schiffer

Originally published in 1932, this wonderful book was sadly limited to a short press run of only 1,200 copies. Though reprinted much later by a commercial press in New York, the original quality of the photographic images was badly compromised. This edition brings back the original *Early Architecture of Delaware* in all its stunning detail.

The cover image is the Van Dyke House, Ken L. Henderson, photographer, 1958, from the collection of the New Castle Historical Society, New Castle, DE.

Copyright © 2006 by Schiffer Publishing, Ltd.
Library of Congress Control Number: 2006923546

Designed by "Sue"

ISBN: 0-7643-2510-8
Printed in China

Published by Schiffer Publishing Ltd.
4880 Lower Valley Road
Atglen, PA 19310
Phone: (610) 593-1777; Fax: (610) 593-2002
E-mail: Info@schifferbooks.com

For the largest selection of fine reference books on this and related subjects, please visit our web site at
www.schifferbooks.com
We are always looking for people to write books on new and related subjects. If you have an idea for a book please contact us at the above address.

This book may be purchased from the publisher.
Include $3.95 for shipping.
Please try your bookstore first.
You may write for a free catalog.

In Europe, Schiffer books are distributed by
Bushwood Books
6 Marksbury Ave.
Kew Gardens
Surrey TW9 4JF England
Phone: 44 (0) 20 8392-8585; Fax: 44 (0) 20 8392-9876
E-mail: info@bushwoodbooks.co.uk
Website: www.bushwoodbooks.co.uk
Free postage in the U.K., Europe; air mail at cost.

To My Wife

ELIZABETH JONES BENNETT

Wm Penn

Quaker Gentlman; who landed
in America, at the old towne of
New Castle on the Dela-
ware, on the day of October
the Twenty-eighth, one thous-
and, six hundred & eighty-two.

CONTENTS

Introduction

GEORGE F. BENNETT'S *Early Architecture of Delaware* is a comprehensive study in the form of photographs and detailed drawings, mostly domestic, which show the influence of successive Dutch, Swedish, and English colonization of the first of these United States.

These present-standing buildings cover a long period of time—1660 to 1840—and a very wide range of style and type. The stately Georgian dwellings of Dover and New Castle, including many hitherto unpublished, are supplemented by scores of those smaller dwellings—of characteristic Delaware brick, stone and frame, wealthy in architectural detail—in which the average man of that day lived out his life.

The book grew out of Mr. Bennett's interest in the architecture of his native State, an interest inspired by the desire to express something beyond the commonplace in the practice of his profession. In the course of innumerable journeys he visited every "hundred" (township in other states) of Delaware; penetrated to the out-of-the-way villages and country by-ways often closed to the stranger and caused to be photographed those buildings and architectural details representative of the State's distinctive early architecture.

Architects, to whom the small house is always a problem, should be especially interested in the fact that so much time and effort have been given to a reproduction of details of the smaller dwellings and domestic buildings; and also the fact that few of the houses shown had previous publication.

JOSEPH L. COPELAND

PAOLI, PENNA., APRIL, 1952.

[9]

Foreword

IT is to be regretted that illustrations of all the fine old houses in the state could not have been included in this volume. We of course made every effort to illustrate representative types of the various periods and on pages 13-14 we have listed a number of places visited which are not illustrated although these houses not only have merit architecturally but are rich in historical background. For example, we selected the Newcastle "Court House" but not the State House in Dover—another example, the home of Commodore McDonough of 1812 fame —still another, the Clayton house (Buena Vista) on the State Road, a fine example of the early 19th century period.

We take this opportunity of thanking the owners of the houses for their many courtesies and genuine interest in our work and to many others for their assistance in various ways. We are especially indebted to Earl Brooks who made all the photographs, to Stanley M. Arthurs for so kindly allowing us to reproduce his painting of Old Swedes Church as a frontispiece, Brandt H. Alexander for decorations, and to Paul L. Hildebrand and associates, Philadelphia. A special word of appreciation is due Horace F. Temple, Inc. of West Chester, Pa., for their tireless efforts and whole-hearted co-operation in the printing and binding.

For invaluable assistance, direct and indirect, and above all for their encouragement, we wish to extend our appreciation to the following: C. Douglas Buck, E. William Martin, Chas. M. Curtis, Norman P. Rood, Thos. F. Bayard, Miss Anna T. Lincoln, Christopher L. Ward, George A. Elliott, John W. McComb, John P. Hyatt, Theo. M. Marvin, James J. O'Neil, Arthur L. Bailey, all of Wilmington, Daniel Corbit of Odessa, Richard S. Rodney and Francis McIntyre of Newcastle, the Society of the Colonial Dames in Delaware and the Historical Society of Delaware.

G. F. B.

Early buildings not included in this volume, with historical notations compiled by the Society of Colonial Dames in Delaware

THE "TUSSEY" HOUSE ON PENNY HILL. EARLY METHODIST MEETING PLACE.

OLD BUILDINGS of University of Delaware, Newark.

CENTRE FRIENDS MEETING HOUSE, 1795, at Yorklyn.

COOCH MANSION, Cooch's Bridge. Lord Howe's Headquarters.

THE JOSIAH LEWDON HOUSE, Newport, 1770.

THE RICHARDSON HOUSE, 1765, on the Newport Pike about a mile from Wilmington, built by Richard Richardson.

ANOTHER RICHARDSON house back from the Pike near Mill "Race" was built in 1723.

THE BANK OF DELAWARE BUILDING, corner Sixth and Market Streets, Wilmington.

FRIENDS' MEETING HOUSE. Fourth and West Streets, Wilmington. Built in 1818. In the graveyard is buried John Dickinson, born 1732, a President of the State of Delaware. A signer of the Constitution and author of the famous "Farmer's Letters."

JOSEPH TATNALL HOUSE. 1803 Market Street. Built 1770. Anthony Wayne's headquarters. Washington came here daily to hold council with Wayne, Lafayette and other officers before the battle of Brandywine. After that battle it was occupied by British Officers. Joseph Tatnall owned and operated the original flour mills on the Brandywine.

"THE SIGN OF THE SHIP." Old tavern S. E. corner Third and Market Sts. Named later "Happy Retreat", now a store.

JACQUETTE HOUSE, 1763, called "Long Hook." Jean Paul Jacquette lived on this tract 1684. Washington and Lafayette often visited here and the house was at all times a social center.

On the Hares Corner Road just beyond the marshes was and is the ANDREW'S PLACE called "Stockford." It was the residence of Col. John Stockton, of the Revolutionary army, and of Gen. James Henry Wilson of Civil War fame.

NICHOLAS VAN DYKE HOUSE, Hares Corner Road. Called the "Hermitage."

MANSION HOUSE, River Road and Hamburg Lane, built by Col. Alex Porter in 1750 (now the Rodney Farm).

On the State Road north of Red Lion, BUENA VISTA, country place built by John M. Clayton, U. S. Senator and Secretary of State under President Taylor, 1846.

PORT PENN, the oldest house Dutch Colonial, date unknown and the Stewart House, built 1728 having cannon ball in walls from the British vessel "Roebuck."

McDONOUGH, original name "The Trap." Home and family burying ground of Commodore McDonough, hero 1812. Kirkwood lived here, the hero of thirty-two battles of the Revolutionary War.

DILWORTH HOUSE, near Augustine Pier, on road from McDonough to Port Penn.

LISTON CORNER HOUSE, 1680. Visited by Pirates 1747.

FAIRVIEW, on Causeway east of Odessa, residence of Elias N. Moore, 1773.

HUGUENOT HOUSE, also known as Dower House, built 1738 by Arnold Naudain.

MANOR HOUSE, built by Edmund Cantwell 1770.

CHRIST CHURCH, Dover. First Church 1708. Present Church 1734. Restora-ations made in 1913-16.

NICHOLAS LOOCKERMAN HOUSE, built for his son Vincent, in 1746. Contains much fine paneling and wood carving. Dover.

PLEASANTON ABBEY, near Dover. North of Silver Lake, on Leipsic Road. Built by Henry Stevens, where he resided during Revolution. An ardent Tory. He concealed British soliders in his house upon several occasions.

CHERBOURG. Three miles east of Dover on Little Creek Road. Deeded to John Marim in 1715. Inherited by his grandson, John Marim, a lieutenant in Col. Patterson's regiment of Dela. troops, Revolutionary War. Home of Cornelius P. Comegy's, Lieutenant Colonel in the War of 1812, Governor of Delaware 1837 to 1841.

SAMUEL DICKINSON HOUSE. Originally called "Kingston-upon-Hull." Slave burying ground, where 400 are said to be interred. Land was part of Logan tract, containing one thousand acres and nine or ten brick dwellings, most of which are of generous size and date back to early days. The most notable on the tract is Towne Point, on the St. Jones Creek, with view of Creek and Bay. Here the first Courts in Kent County were held.

CAESAR RODNEY HOUSE, Byefield, a tract of nine hundred acres, taken up in 1680 and inherited by Caesar Rodney from his father William. This was the home to which he returned after making his famous ride. Qaint staircase of small proportions, but very delicate. Long low building with dominating dormers.

COOPER'S CORNER HOUSE, early 18th century. Near Camden, originally called Piccadilly by Daniel Mifflin, the first settler, then changed to Mifflin's Cross Roads. In 1788 became known as Camden.

DANIEL MIFFLIN HOUSE. Built 1783.

BARRATT'S CHAPEL. One mile north of Frederica on State Road. "Cradle of Methodism in America." Here Bishop Thomas Coke and Francis Asbury met, and arranged the preliminaries for the Methodist Episcopal Church. Here too, sacramental ordinances were first administered in America by authorized Methodist preachers. Old brick meeting house with burial ground, including about 18 acres, built 1780.

RINGGOLD HOUSE, near Kenton.

BYRN ZION BAPTIST CHURCH, near Kenton, built 1781.

HOUSE at N. W. Corner of First and Market Sts., Georgetown, called "The Judge's." Built by Judge Peter Robinson about 1810.

OLD CHRIST CHURCH, Broad Creek, Founded 1707. Two miles east of Laurel. Interesting interior.

EARLY ARCHITECTURE OF DELAWARE

THE SWEDES ON DELAWARE

THE Swedish colonists following in the wake of the men who landed at the mouth of Christiana river in 1638 to establish the brief Swedish sovereignty on the Delaware, left few records in architecture for later generations to study. Nowhere within the State is to be found a trace of the high-roofed, many gabled wooden houses and churches of the northern kingdom of that day; nor is there record of such buildings. A few log houses attributed to the Swedes, built in the late seventeenth century, remain, but they are far from Scandinavian in arrangement or exterior design. Nor are they English. They are American.

Growing out of a need for shelter rather than an appreciation of design, these houses were built on lines as simple and straightforward as were the lives of the people. The farming folk who built them, with the help of neighbors and, possibly, a country carpenter, were likely to be of native birth, first or second generation Americans with a hearty appreciation of the opportunities of the new land and a growing disregard for things European. They were not tied by tradition, and the houses they lived in grew naturally from the elemental need of civilized man for four walls, a roof and a hearthstone. Erected more carefully and in more leisurely fashion than the rude cabins of the first settlers, they remain to this day—somewhat altered by the needs and wishes of succeeding generations—to remind us that the earliest permanent settlers of Delaware were simple, homely folk whose taste and means ran to cottages, not castles.

By the middle of the following century their descendents were living on a far higher plane. Israel Acrelius, provost of the Swedish churches in America, writing at Stockholm in 1758 after his return to Sweden, says: "The houses are built of bricks, after the English fashion, without coating, every other brick glazed; or they are of sandstone, granite, etc., as is mostly the case in the country. Sometimes also they are built of oak planks five inches thick. To build of wood is not regarded as economy, after everything is paid for. The roof is of cedar shingles. Within, the walls and ceilings are plastered, and whitewashed once a year. . . . The windows are large, divided into two pieces, the upper and lower; the latter is opened by raising and shut by lowering. The woodwork is painted, or it does not last long."

That was in the middle of the eighteenth century, however, and by that time the English influence was paramount. Less than thirty years after Acrelius wrote, congregations of the Swedish churches could no longer understand the language of pastors sent from Sweden and so broke a contact with the Swedish Throne that had lasted for almost a century. Having become assimilated with their English neighbors, marriages between the two peoples being frequent, the Swedes likewise accepted the excellent architectural forms brought into the country from England and built accordingly, but with that adherence to local practice that sets the early houses of Delaware apart from those of neighboring colonies.

Gallery Entrance—South Porch   *Added 1751*

HOLY TRINITY (OLD SWEDES) CHURCH, WILMINGTON
Original church erected 1698-99

South Porch   *1751*

There is one architectural achievement that stands out in the early record of the Swedes on Delaware, however; and behind that achievement, giving it form, carrying it forward to fruition, stands the now shadowy and almost forgotten figure of a man. Holy Trinity Church (Old Swedes) in Wilmington, the "Church at Christina" of old records, has been in almost continuous use as a place of worship since 1699; and pleasantly haunting it is the ghostly figure of the man who built it, the young pastor, Eric Bjork, who caused to be placed on the west exterior wall these words: "If God be for us, who can be against us."

Pastor Bjork, or, as he was known in moments of dignity, Honorworthy Sir Magister Ericus Biork, has been dead and laid to rest in his native Sweden these many years, but the story of the building of Holy Trinity as told in his own words presents him to us as such a dominating figure of living, forceful manhood that it is probably incorrect to refer to him in any sense as ghostly. He seems to have put into those walls as the masons laid them up stone by stone some of that fine spiritual quality that uplifted him from the men around him, a quality of great love and deeply purposeful religion. But with it all he was a man of action, a straightforward, forceful, dominating sort of man who had a church built and consecrated while the Swedes at Wiccaco were quarreling about a location.

He was a man of orderly mind and systematic habits and put down in his book from day to day those things that had to do with the building of the church. And so we come to this bit in a long list of things to be given attention at the earliest moment: "To get again from Hans Pietterson the Bell which he maliciously . . . lied out from the man in whose care it was left at Marcus Hook, which bell was given us by Captain Trent when he went away."

The subject does not appear again and one wonders if the original church bell, which is said to have hung from the limb of a walnut tree at the west end of the church, was a ship's bell which a certain churchwarden coveted and made away with. Knowing Eric Bjork, we assume that it was; that Hans Pietterson gave in as gracefully as possible. It was not the first time this churchwarden had aroused the ire of his pastor, nor was it to be the last.

Eric Bjork, sent from Sweden as a missionary-priest of the Lutheran Church, arrived in America at the end of June, 1697. Within a few days he met with the congregation of Crane Hook Church, near New-castle, and within the

South Elevation of Tower   *Added 1802*

month had it meet to "choose certain discreet persons . . . to act for the whole congregation in selecting and agreeing upon a place where we in Jesus' name should set our new church." Christina—the present Wilmington—was agreed upon and months of preparation and discussion followed, but on May 28 of the following year the first stones of the foundation were "laid all around about one foot deep except a piece on the south wall." And so the building of the church was under way.

Joseph Yard, from Philadelphia, and his three sons, Joseph, William and John, were the masons. For the sum of eighty-six pounds, silver money, he agreed "with the help of God to lay all the stone and Brick work of a church . . . at Christeen near John Stallcop's; the length of it shall be 66 foot from out to out, the breath shall be 36 foot from out to out, and to be laid in ye ground, a good and firm foundation, and the height from ye Topp of ye ground upwards 20 foot, and ye thickness of ye wall from ye foundation to the lower ends of the windows 3 foot thick, and then afterwards 2 foot thick upwards, and all ye Windows and doors upon the Church shall be Arched, and the doors and Windows Arched and Quined with Bricks . . ."

Interior view Southdoor and Gallery Platform

HOLY TRINITY (OLD SWEDES) CHURCH, WILMINGTON

so that the arch in the church is in danger of breaking; the wall can be made so as to serve as a protection in stormy weather and from the heat of summer. The roof was found much decayed. The bell needs recasting, having been cracked for many years. The church should be rid of the nests of birds which are built under the arch over the pews. The north and west doors which are entirely decayed should be made anew."

This work was apparently done in the summer of 1751, for reference is made by Herr Acrelius in 1753 of payment having been made for the "side arches of the church." A note by the translator is to the effect that these arches were built in 1740, although no reference to them seems to appear in the church records. At all events, it is believed that the present arched porch on the south side of the church edifice was built about the middle of the eighteenth century and, no doubt, the work was carried out under the energetic direction of Israel Acrelius, who seems to have been the only pastor since Bjork to have taken such interest in the church at Christina.

Returning to that earlier time, one finds Pastor Bjork vigorously pushing forward the work on the church during the winter of 1698 and the spring of 1699. John Harrison, an expert joiner from Philadelphia, had been engaged to help Smart in place of the "comrade" who failed him. To John Harrison had been assigned "all ye Inside work . . . that is all ye pews and Windows, shot work and the Pulpit with a canape over it and a pew of each side of ye communion Table and also with Reals and Banisters about ye church . . . and finish all the Sealing Joice which is to doe and fitt In ye sealing of ye Roof . . . and to doe with plained Boards over ye three doors In ye church where it is left undone."

All this was necessary because John Smart, deserted by Britt and left alone with heavy work, fell ill and the work lagged. Eventually another John, a Quaker named Davis, came down to help and then came John Harrison and between them and aid given by members of the congregation most of the roof was on by Christmas of 1698. Eric Bjork was pleased with Harrison's workmanship and when the joiner and John Smart quarreled about money, the minister made up the difference out of his own pocket in order that the work might go forward. Later on he was to go into his pocket again and make up a sum of one hundred and thirty-five pounds, eight shillings and sixpence to clear off the remaining debt against the building that "it seems safe to say", he writes, "in round numbers, as it now within a year (Glory be to God) is come to be finished, has cost 800 pounds Pennsylvania currency."

Eventually the day came when the whole was finished. Mattias de Foss, a smith—and the only skilled workman among the Swedish people engaged upon the work, so far as the church records show—had made letters and numerals of wrought iron for the inscriptions on north, south, east and west walls. Trinity Sunday came on June 4 that year and a few days before that date Joseph Yard Jr. came down from Philadelphia, cleaned the west gable of mortar and dirt and colored with red lead the date and long inscription in queer Latin abbreviations that tells how the church was built "in the reign of William III, by Grace of God, King of England, William Penn, Proprietor, Vice Governor William Markham, the Most Illustrious King of the Swedes Charles XI, now of most glorious memory, having sent here Ericus Tobias Biork of Westmania, Pastor Loci."

It is not likely that many of the congregation which filed solemnly into the church on that first hot Sunday morning of the consecration, could understand the inscription in the wall above their heads. But one hopes that Pastor Bjork took occasion to translate at least one line of it, that line bold with faith which reads

If God Be For Us, Who Can Be Against Us?

Not a bad rallying cry for any man or any church or any nation in these days when faith seems to have left the hearts of the people and mankind throughout the world is sunk in a slough of despond.

April, 1932.

The interior has never been painted, and the fine panelled woodwork is chestnut brown in color

Detail of Gallery platform framing

PRINCE GEORGE'S CHAPEL, DAGSBORO HUNDRED
Mentioned in letters as early as 1717, and presumably was built about that time. It was enlarged about 1750, these illustrations are of the original part, however.

The gallery is reached by two stairways each about 30" wide, the steps are very steep with a rise of 9½" and 7½" tread
PRINCE GEORGE'S CHAPEL, DAGSBORO HUNDRED

Detail of Pulpit   *1773*

OLD DRAWYER'S. ST. GEORGE'S HUNDRED

East front elevation

OLD DRAWYERS

SCOTS and Irish Protestants appeared early in the settlement of Delaware and by the late seventeenth century were there in sufficient numbers to form two Presbyterian congregations, one at New Castle and the other on Drawyers Creek, near Odessa. In an address delivered at an historical celebration some ninety years ago, the Rev. George Foot, then pastor of Old Drawyers, said he believed the congregation was organized previous to 1700. The first church was of frame, possibly of log or hewn timber construction. It was enlarged several times, once in 1736.

The present building, one of the finer surviving examples of eighteenth century meeting house architecture, was erected in 1773. It is as stiffly and uncompromisingly Protestant in its lines as were the backs of the men who caused it to be built. Nowhere, within or without, can be found any concession to religious practices more soft, more alluring, more colorful than the preaching and psalm-singing of the followers of Calvin and John Knox.

No belfry, no steeple breaks the rigid line of the roof tree; no altar bright with candles suggests a less stern form of worship. A pulpit five steps up from the floor of the church provides a reading desk for the convenience of the minister and a narrow and, at best, uncomfortable bench for him to sit upon. Below his reading desk is the railed-in enclosure and desk for the precentor. The remainder of the lower floor is given over to pews; the gallery, stepped up sharply, is filled with even more uncompromising seats of unpainted pine.

If that were all that could be said for Old Drawyers Church it would be of no value to say so little. But greater things can be said. If there was no altar, there was, at least, simple Communion; if there were no candles, there was the sunlight streaming in through many windows; if there was no ritual, there was a man to preach God on Sabbath mornings. No house in which generations of men and women have lived together in joy and harmony can ever be altogether quit of their happy ghosts; no church in which man has opened his heart to divine love and guidance over a period of years can ever be closed long enough to let that spiritual quality evaporate. And here in Old Drawyers one is at once aware of the spiritual presence of those dour men and women of Protestant Ireland and Protestant Scotland whose outward sternness so often concealed hearts quick to sympathize and hands quick to help.

Front Entrance   *Side doorway*

OLD DRAWYER'S CHURCH, ST. GEORGE'S HUNDRED

Stairway to gallery

Gallery rail

Pews—north wall—1st floor

OLD DRAWYER'S CHURCH, ST. GEORGE'S HUNDRED.
See Part II for large scale profiles

Box pews—gallery—north wall

Bench pews—gallery—south wall

OLD DRAWYER'S CHURCH, ST. GEORGE'S HUNDRED

FRIENDS' MEETING HOUSE, CAMDEN   *1806*

Front Doorway

EARLY ARCHITECTURE OF DELAWARE

MEMBERS of the Society of Friends were settled in Brandywine Hundred as early as 1682 and before long their modest meeting houses began to appear here and there in the three counties. A meeting house was built in New Castle in 1705 and in 1738 the first brick meeting house of the Society was built on West street, near Fourth, in the then new town of Wilmington. In the same year a meeting house was built at Hockessin.

Friends living at Lewes had held meeting there as early as 1692 and it is said the first religious body to hold services at the Duck Creek region was this same Society. Meeting houses were erected there and at Little Creek prior to the Revolution; and a meeting house was erected in 1703 on the road from Port Penn. It was first called Georges Creek Meeting and the site was later occupied by a Friends' burying ground. This meeting is said to have removed to Odessa, where the present small brick meeting house was erected in 1780.

The Friends in Delaware, as elsewhere, were ardent advocates of a liberal education. The Friends' Union Academy at Camden, organized in 1815, was for many years one of the most advanced institutions of learning in the State.

Circa 1780

FRIENDS' MEETING HOUSE, ODESSA
See Part II for details and measured drawings

St. James' Church   *1822*

Detail Gate Post   *North Drive Entrance*

ST. JAMES' CHURCH, NEAR STANTON
See Part II for details of north entrance door

EARLY ARCHITECTURE OF DELAWARE

ST. ANNE'S CHURCH, MIDDLETOWN

ST. Anne's Episcopal Church at Middletown is one of the oldest Episcopal congregations in the State, having been established prior to 1704. The present building is said to have been built in 1768.*

The congregation treasures a fine altar cloth presented by Queen Anne. The cloth is embroidered with the royal monogram, A. R., believed to have been the work of the Queen herself. Architecturally, the building allies itself with those structures erected in the State from 1730 onward to the revolutionary period. It is of two stories, without exterior ornament except a cove cornice and with an interior unmarked by elaborate detail. A fine fanlight window distinguishes it, however.

The first stated pastor was that Rev. Mr. Jenkins referred to by a brother clergyman as "poor Brother Jenkins at Appoquinimink . . . baited to death by mosquitoes and blood-thirsty gal-nippers, which would not let him rest day or night till he got a fever and died of a calenture." Following the demise of unlucky Mr. Jenkins the pastor of the Swedish church at Christiana, the indomitable Eric Bjork, preached to the congregation once a month.

At the time of the Revolution the rector was Rev. Philip Reading, an Englishman loyal to George III. He had served the church for thirty-four years, but on August 25, 1776, closed and locked the doors and the church was not opened again in his lifetime. He died in 1778 and is buried in the churchyard.

*The cove cornice and other details indicate an earlier date; see the Van Dyke House, page 60.

South End Elevation

ST. ANNE'S, NEAR MIDDLETOWN

*Shutters panelled one side—batten boards on back set chevron-wise to form a
herring-bone figure, characteristic of this vicinity*

ST. ANNE'S, NEAR MIDDLETOWN

Built 1740

THE FIRST PRESBYTERIAN CHURCH, WILMINGTON
Now the home of the National Society of Colonial Dames in Delaware

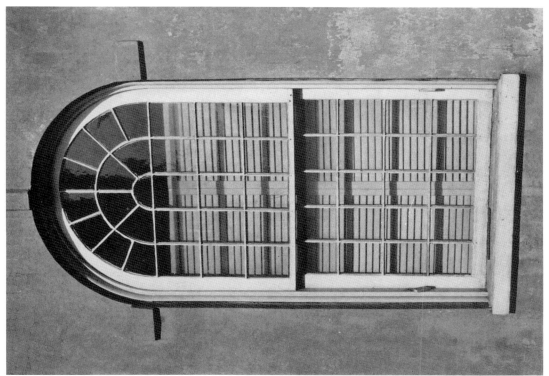

Detail of Window

IMMANUEL CHURCH, NEW CASTLE

The details shown are part of changes made about 1820

First English Church on Delaware (1704)

Side Entrance

ST. GEORGE'S CHURCH
On South side of Love's Branch, about nine miles from Lewes

1794

OLD PRESBYTERIAN CHURCH, NEW CASTLE

Circa 1707

Detail of Cupola   *Circa 1840*

SCHOOL HOUSE, ODESSA

1798

BRANDYWINE ACADEMY, WILMINGTON

Circa 1798

OLD TOWN HALL, WILMINGTON

Built about 1820

Detail of Cupola

TOWN HALL, NEW CASTLE

Detail of Cupola

COURT HOUSE (formerly State House) NEW CASTLE

Stairway—South Terrace

HOUSE NEAR CORNER KETCH

House Facing Dover Green

House near Yorklyn

SMALL HOUSES

House on Riverfront—near New Castle

House on Old Wilmington-New Castle Road

SMALL HOUSES

EARLY ARCHITECTURE OF DELAWARE

Near Smyrna

Duck Creek

Old Wilmington-New Castle Road

DETAILS—SMALL HOUSES

Lewes

Lewes

DETAILS—SMALL HOUSES

Old Law Office, Smyrna

Lewes

Lewes

SMALL HOUSES

Odessa

Lewes

Centerville

Yorklyn

DETAILS—SMALL HOUSES

Newport

HOUSES WITH PENT EAVE

Near Marshallton

Newport

Near Marshallton   *Christiana*

HOUSES WITH PENT EAVE

East Elevation

HOUSE IN WHICH NICHOLAS VAN DYKE SR. LIVED, NEW CASTLE

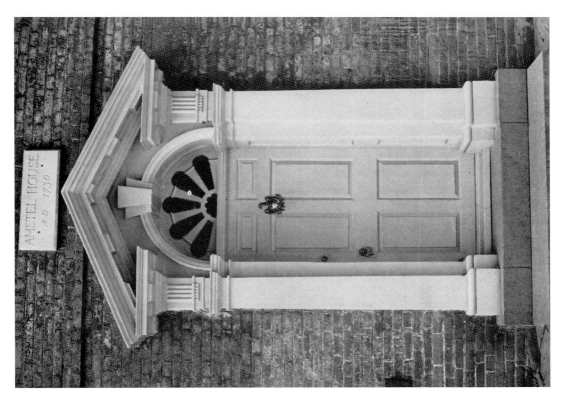

HOUSE IN WHICH NICHOLAS VAN DYKE SR. LIVED, NEW CASTLE

Panelling in Living Room

HOUSE IN WHICH NICHOLAS VAN DYKE SR. LIVED, NEW CASTLE

See Part II for large scale profiles

Living Room

HOUSE IN WHICH NICHOLAS VAN DYKE SR. LIVED, NEW CASTLE

Panelling in Room—2nd Floor

HOUSE IN WHICH NICHOLAS VAN DYKE SR. LIVED, NEW CASTLE

See Part II for drawings

South Elevation

Fire-place in Block House

ROBINSON HOUSE (NAAMANS) BRANDYWINE HUNDRED

Detail—Room on Second Floor

"Block House" built about the middle of the 17th century

East Elevation

ROBINSON HOUSE
(NAAMANS)
BRANDYWINE HUNDRED

See Part II for drawing and large scale profiles

GRANTHAM HOUSE

FROM HOUSE ON RIVER FRONT NEAR NEW CASTLE

River Front, New Castle

River Front near Wilmington

Leipsic

Odessa

DETAILS—SMALL HOUSES

Near Hockessin

Near Duck Creek   *Near Canterbury*

SMALL HOUSES

Near New Castle

Odessa

Douglas House, near Canterbury

DETAILS—SMALL HOUSES

HOUSE IN CHRISTIANA
See Part II for large scale profiles

*Original House
Circa 1765* | *Addition about 1795*

North Entrance *South Porch*

HENRY LATIMER HOUSE, NEAR NEWPORT
See Part II for large scale drawings and profiles

South Elevation

HENRY LATIMER HOUSE NEAR NEWPORT

THE VAN LEUVENIGH HOUSE
The Strand, New Castle

Panelling in Living Room—see Part II for drawing

THE VAN LEUVENIGH HOUSE
The Strand, New Castle

THE WILSON HOUSE, ODESSA
See Part II for details and measured drawings

Panelling in Dining Room

Stair Hall

WILSON HOUSE, ODESSA
See Part II for measured drawings

Detail—Stairway Second Floor Level

WILSON HOUSE, ODESSA

Main Facade

CORBIT HOUSE, ODESSA

Detail—South Elevation

CORBIT HOUSE, ODESSA
See Part II for details

Blinds Closed

CORBIT HOUSE, ODESSA

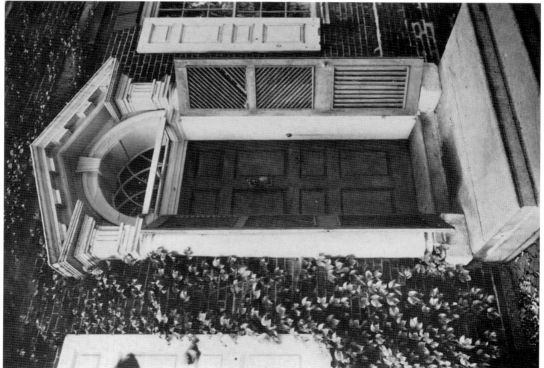

Entrance Door—Blinds Open

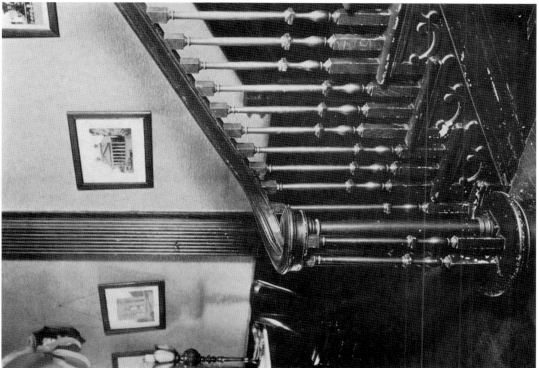

Detail—Stairway

Main Stair Hall

CORBIT HOUSE, ODESSA

Detail—Reception Room

Detail—Reception Room

CORBIT HOUSE, ODESSA

Mantel Detail—Reception Room

CORBIT HOUSE, ODESSA

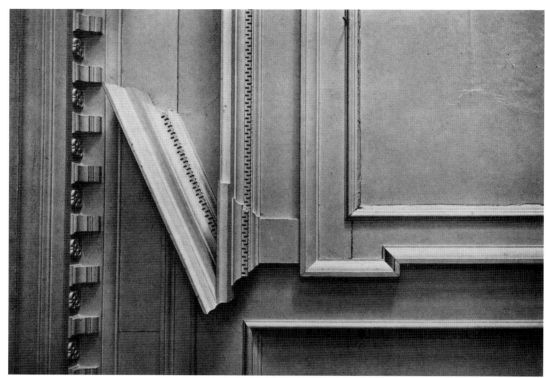

Detail—"Over Mantel" Reception Room

CORBIT HOUSE, ODESSA

Detail Around Window—Reception Room

Detail of Entrance

THE KENSEY-JOHNS HOUSE, NEW CASTLE

Stair Hall

THE KENSEY-JOHNS HOUSE, NEW CASTLE
See Part II for large scale profiles

Mantel—Living Room

THE KENSEY-JOHNS HOUSE, NEW CASTLE
See Part II for details and measured drawings

THE KENSEY-JOHNS HOUSE, NEW CASTLE
See Part II for details and measured drawings

Panelling in Dining Room

THE STRAND, NEW CASTLE

CHIEF JUSTICE BOOTH HOUSE, NEW CASTLE

MANTELS—NEW CASTLE

The Charles Thomas House, New Castle

Main Facade

THE VAN DYKE HOUSE, 400 DELAWARE ST., NEW CASTLE

Blinds Closed

Entrance Door—Blinds Open

THE VAN DYKE HOUSE, 400 DELAWARE ST., NEW CASTLE

HOUSE AT No. 18 ORANGE ST., NEW CASTLE

Stairway

THE CHARLES THOMAS HOUSE

Cellar Window—New Castle

Cellar Window—New Castle

Near Middletown

DETAILS—SMALL HOUSES

On River Front, near New Castle

DETAILS—SMALL HOUSES

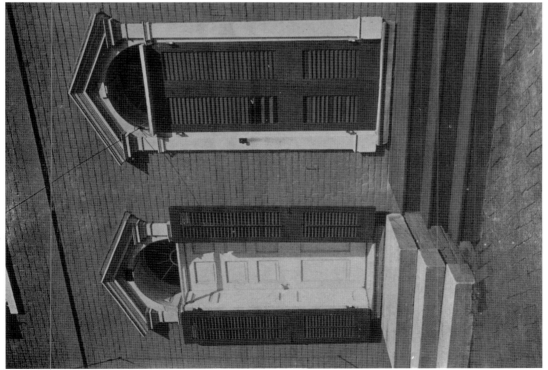

On the Strand, New Castle

New Castle

Near Middletown

Odessa

The Strand, New Castle

DETAILS—SMALL HOUSES

Dormer

GEORGE READ II HOUSE, NEW CASTLE

Garden Entrance Detail

THE GEORGE READ II HOUSE, NEW CASTLE

Detail of Front

THE GEORGE READ II HOUSE
The Strand, New Castle

THE GEORGE READ II HOUSE, THE STRAND, NEW CASTLE

Detail of Palladian Window—see page 127 for interior detail

THE GEORGE READ II HOUSE, THE STRAND, NEW CASTLE

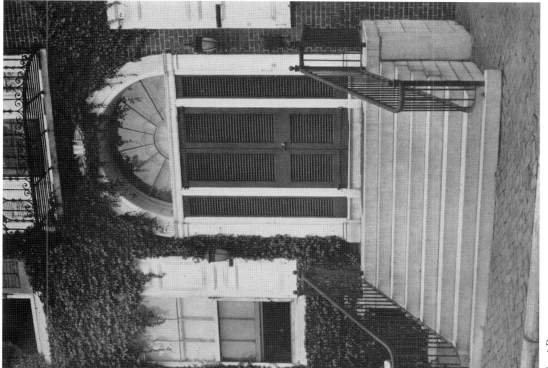

Front Doorway

Entrance Hall

THE GEORGE READ II HOUSE, NEW CASTLE
See Part II for details of doorway

Entrance Hall

THE GEORGE READ II HOUSE, NEW CASTLE

Details of Main Stairway—First Floor

THE GEORGE READ II HOUSE NEW CASTLE
See Part II for large scale profiles

Main Stair Hall

THE GEORGE READ II HOUSE, NEW CASTLE

Reception Room

THE GEORGE READ II HOUSE, NEW CASTLE

Mantel in Reception Room

THE GEORGE READ II HOUSE, NEW CASTLE
See Part II for large scale drawings

Doorway between Reception and Living Rooms

Detail of Mantel in Reception Room

THE GEORGE READ II HOUSE, NEW CASTLE

See Part II for large scale drawings

Details of Doorway between Reception and Living Rooms

THE GEORGE READ II HOUSE, NEW CASTLE
See Part II for large scale drawings

Doorway between Reception and Living Rooms

THE GEORGE READ II HOUSE, NEW CASTLE
See Part II for measured drawings

Dining Room

THE GEORGE READ II HOUSE, NEW CASTLE

Detail—Doorway on second floor

Detail of Stairway—second floor level

THE GEORGE READ II HOUSE, NEW CASTLE

Interior Detail of Palladian Window—2nd Floor
For Exterior see page 115

THE GEORGE READ II HOUSE, NEW CASTLE

Stairway 3rd Floor to "Captain's Walk"

Detail Main Stairway—3rd Floor Level

THE GEORGE READ II HOUSE, NEW CASTLE
See Part II for large scale profiles

Details—2nd Floor "Drawing Room"

Details of Stairway   *Detail at Third Floor Level*

THE GEORGE READ II HOUSE, NEW CASTLE

St. George's Hundred

New Castle

DETAILS—SMALL HOUSES

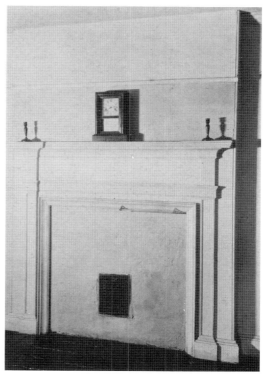

MANTELS—NEW CASTLE

STAIRWAYS—NEW CASTLE

Mantels—New Castle

Mantels—New Castle

DETAILS—SMALL HOUSES

North Elevation

"WOODBURNE", DOVER

Main Entrance Door—Interior

"WOODBURNE", DOVER

Main Entrance Door

Stair Hall

"WOODBURNE", DOVER

Stair Hall—Second Floor

Detail—First Floor   *Detail—Second Floor*

"WOODBURNE", DOVER

Dining Room

"WOODBURNE", DOVER

Room on Second Floor

"WOODBURNE", DOVER

Dining Room

Room on Second Floor

"WOODBURNE", DOVER

EARLY ROW TYPE HOUSE, HENRY CLAY

ON RIVER FRONT NEAR NEW CASTLE

HOUSES—(The 1820-1830 Period)—NEW CASTLE

Delaware St. elevation

SENATOR NICHOLAS VAN DYKE HOUSE, NEW CASTLE
(The 1820-1830 Period)

Entrance Hall

SENATOR NICHOLAS VAN DYKE HOUSE, NEW CASTLE
(The 1820-1830 Period)

Detail—Main Stairway

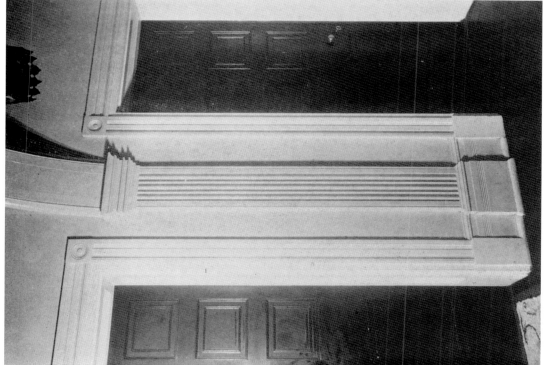

Detail—Entrance Hall

SENATOR NICHOLAS VAN DYKE HOUSE, NEW CASTLE

(The 1820-1830 Period)

Living Room

SENATOR NICHOLAS VAN DYKE HOUSE, NEW CASTLE
(The 1820-1830 Period)

Number 400 Delaware St., New Castle

Senator Nicholas Van Dyke House

House on the Strand

DETAILS—(The 1820-30 Period)—NEW CASTLE

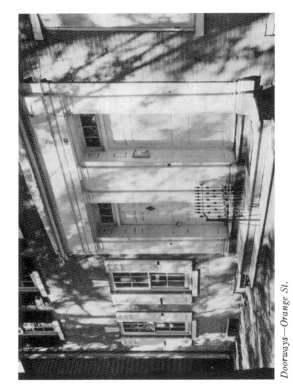

Doorways—Orange St.

Porch—Shop on The Strand

House on The Strand

DETAILS—(The 1820-50 Period)—NEW CASTLE

HOUSE NEAR NEW CASTLE
(The 1820-1830 Period)

Lewes

Duck Creek

TYPICAL SMALL HOUSES IN KENT AND SUSSEX COUNTIES
(The 1820-1840 Period)

Detail—Summer Kitchen

LITTLE CREEK

GRIST MILL—LIMESTONE ROAD NEAR CORNER KETCH

Near Christiana

Burton's Mill—Loves Branch near Lewes

Rockland

Odessa

Odessa

OUT-BUILDINGS

Brandywine Hundred

Hockessin

Christiana

OUT-BUILDINGS

Detail—Spring House

Spring House near Hockessin

OUT-BUILDINGS

Near Middletown

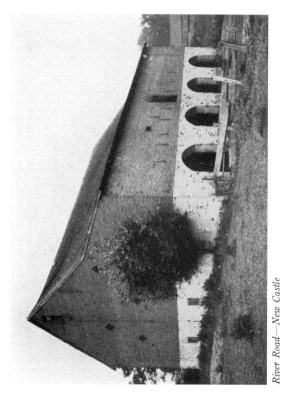

River Road—New Castle

OUT-BUILDINGS

Spring House—Sussex

Ice House—Odessa

OUT-BUILDINGS

Smoke House, near Centerville

Near New Castle

Pump Shelter, Old Drawyer's Church Yard

Wagon House, Duck Creek

OUT-BUILDINGS

Odessa

Detail—Lime Kiln

DETAIL—BRIDGE, ROCKLAND

OLD TOWN HALL
WILMINGTON

PART II

Details

Measured Drawings

Profiles

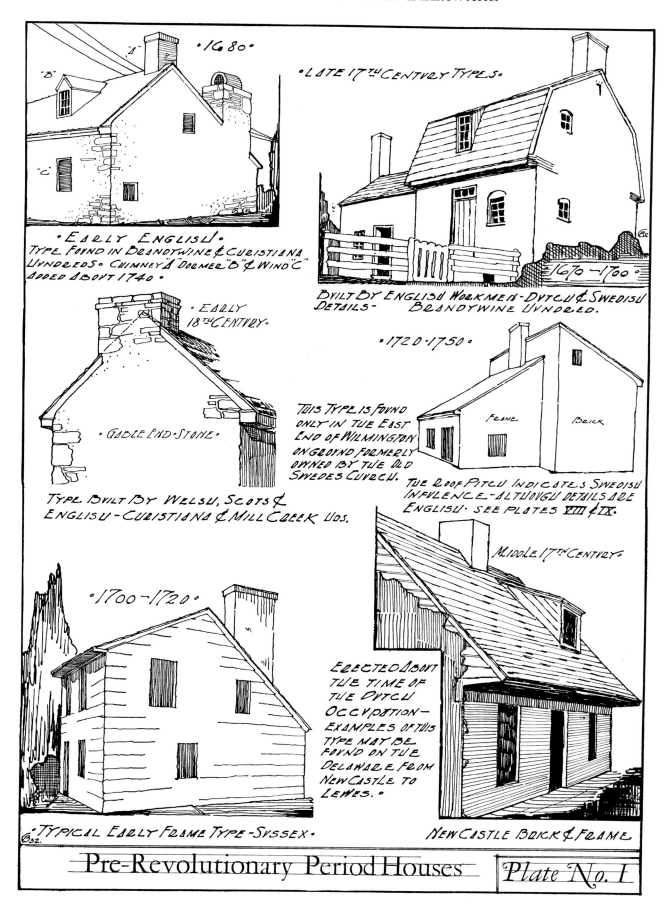

·1680·

·EARLY ENGLISH·
TYPE FOUND IN BRANDYWINE & CHRISTIANA
HUNDREDS· CHIMNEY "A" DORMER "B" & WIND "C"
ADDED ABOUT 1740·

·EARLY
18TH CENTURY·

·GABLE END·STONE·

TYPE BUILT BY WELSH, SCOTS &
ENGLISH - CHRISTIANA & MILL CREEK HDS.

·LATE 17TH CENTURY TYPES·

BUILT BY ENGLISH WORKMEN - DUTCH & SWEDISH
DETAILS - BRANDYWINE HUNDRED.
·1670 - 1700·

·1720 - 1750·

THIS TYPE IS FOUND
ONLY IN THE EAST
END OF WILMINGTON
ON GROUND FORMERLY
OWNED BY THE OLD
SWEDES CHURCH.

FRAME   BRICK

THE ROOF PITCH INDICATES SWEDISH
INFLUENCE - ALTHOUGH DETAILS ARE
ENGLISH· SEE PLATES VIII & IX.

·1700 - 1720·

·TYPICAL EARLY FRAME TYPE - SUSSEX·

MIDDLE 17TH CENTURY·

ERECTED ABOUT
THE TIME OF
THE DUTCH
OCCUPATION —
EXAMPLES OF THIS
TYPE MAY BE
FOUND ON THE
DELAWARE FROM
NEW CASTLE TO
LEWES·

NEW CASTLE BRICK & FRAME

Pre-Revolutionary Period Houses   Plate No. I

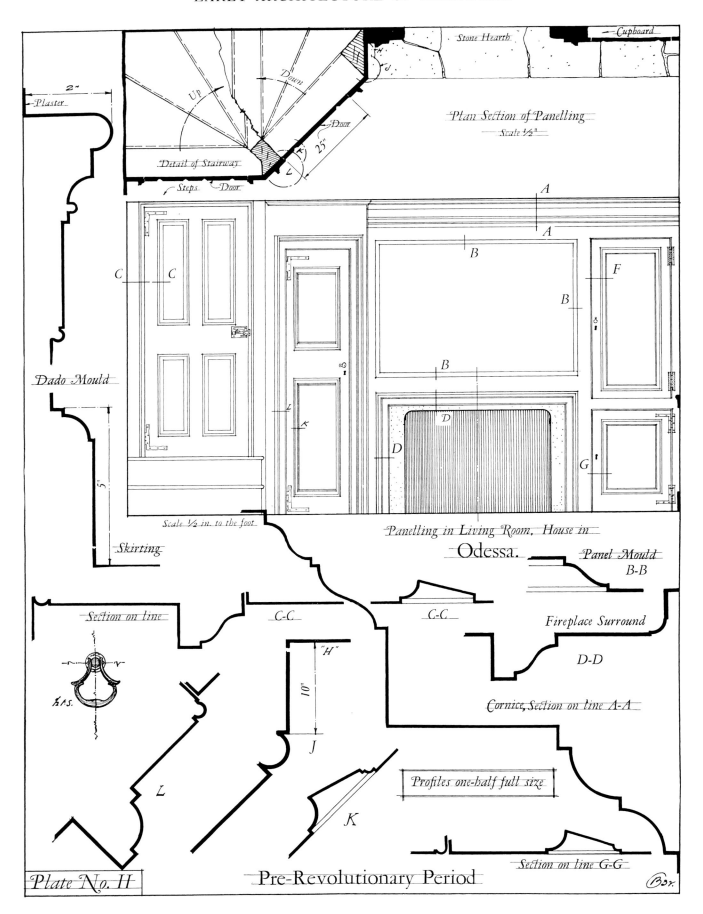

Plan Section of Panelling
—Scale ½"—

Detail of Stairway

Plaster

Dado Mould

Skirting

Scale ½ in. to the foot

Panelling in Living Room, House in
Odessa.

Panel Mould
B-B

Section on line

C-C

C-C

Fireplace Surround
D-D

Cornice, Section on line A-A

Profiles one-half full size

Section on line G-G

Plate No. II

Pre-Revolutionary Period

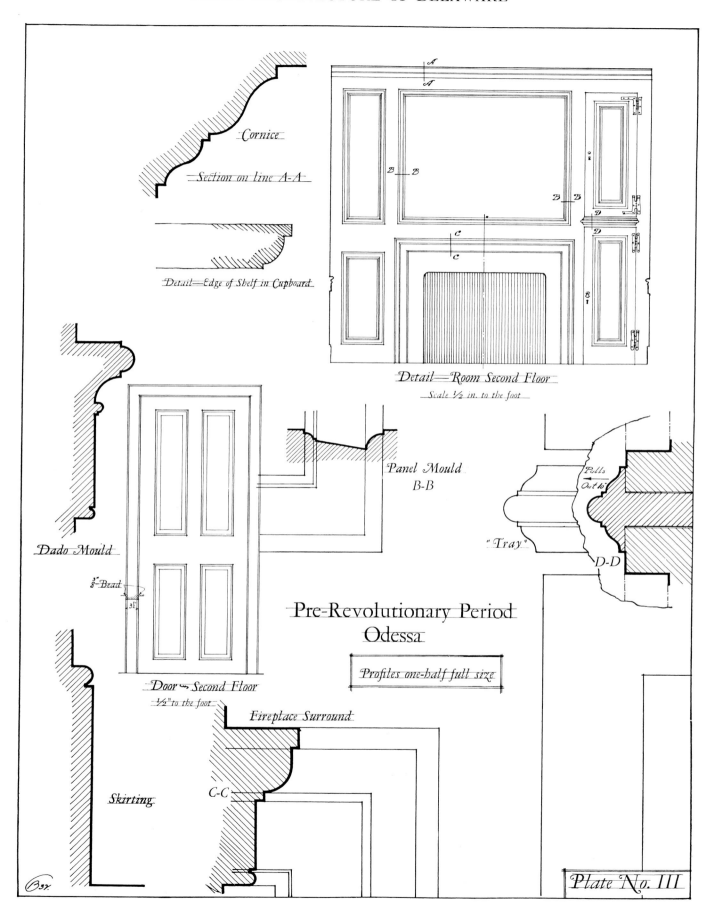

Cornice

Section on line A-A

Detail—Edge of Shelf in Cupboard

Detail—Room Second Floor

Scale ½ in. to the foot

Dado Mould

⅜" Bead

Door — Second Floor

½" to the foot

Panel Mould
B-B

"Tray"

D-D

Pre-Revolutionary Period
Odessa

Profiles one-half full size

Fireplace Surround

C-C

Skirting

Plate No. III

Plate No. IV

See Plate No. V

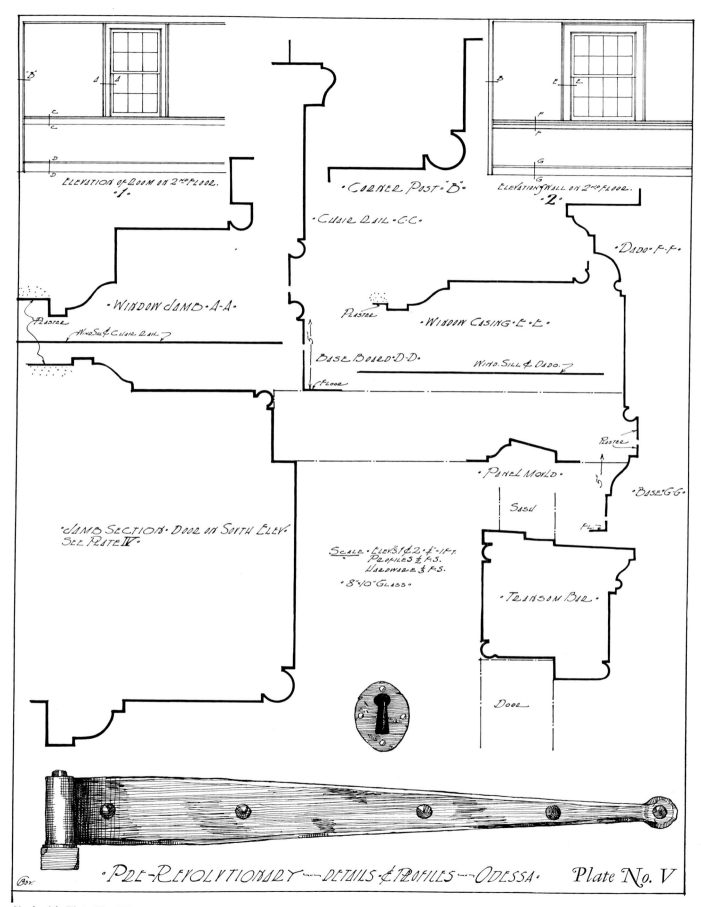

·ELEVATION OF ROOM ON 2ND FLOOR·
·1·

·CORNER POST·"B"·

·CHAIR RAIL·C·C·

·ELEVATION OF WALL ON 2ND FLOOR·
·2·

·WINDOW JAMB·A·A·

PLASTER

WIND. SILL & CHAIR RAIL

PLASTER

·WINDOW CASING·E·E·

·DADO·F·F·

BASE BOARD·D·D·

WIND. SILL & DADO.

FLOOR

·JAMB SECTION·DOOR ON SOUTH ELEV·
·SEE PLATE IV·

·PANEL MO'LD·

PLASTER

·BASE·G·G·

SASH

FL.

·TRANSOM BAR·

·SCALE·ELEVS.1 & 2·¼"=1 FT.
·PROFILES ½ F.S.
·HARDWARE ½ F.S.

·8"×10"GLASS·

DOOR

·PRE-REVOLUTIONARY —— DETAILS & PROFILES —— ODESSA·   Plate No. V

Used with Plate No. IV

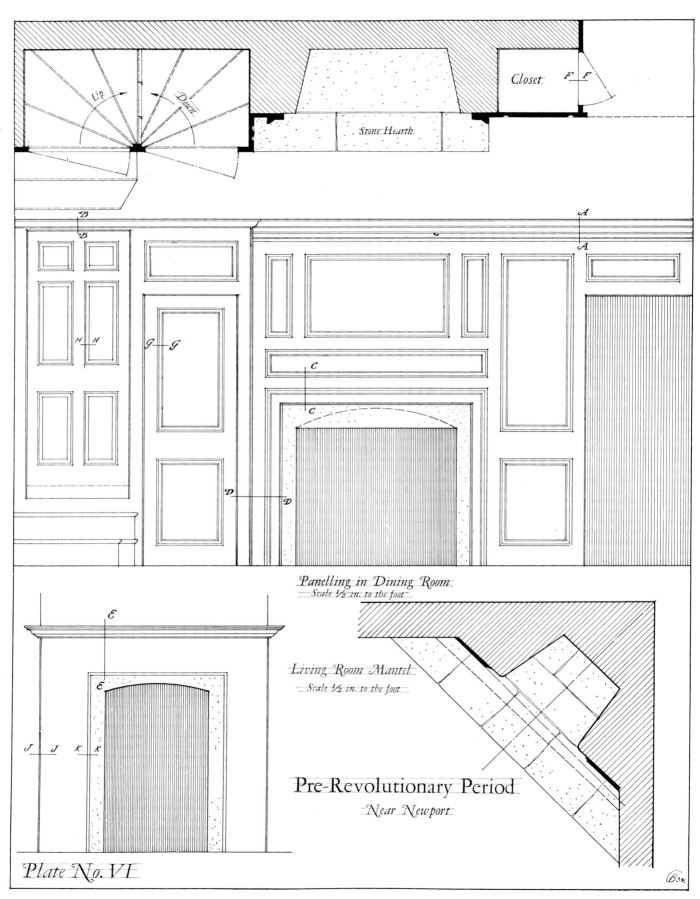

Up

Down

Closet

F F

Stone Hearth

B
B

A
A

C

H H

G G

C
C

D
D

Panelling in Dining Room
Scale ½ in. to the foot

Living Room Mantel
Scale ½ in. to the foot

E
E

J J K K

Pre-Revolutionary Period
Near Newport

Plate No. VI

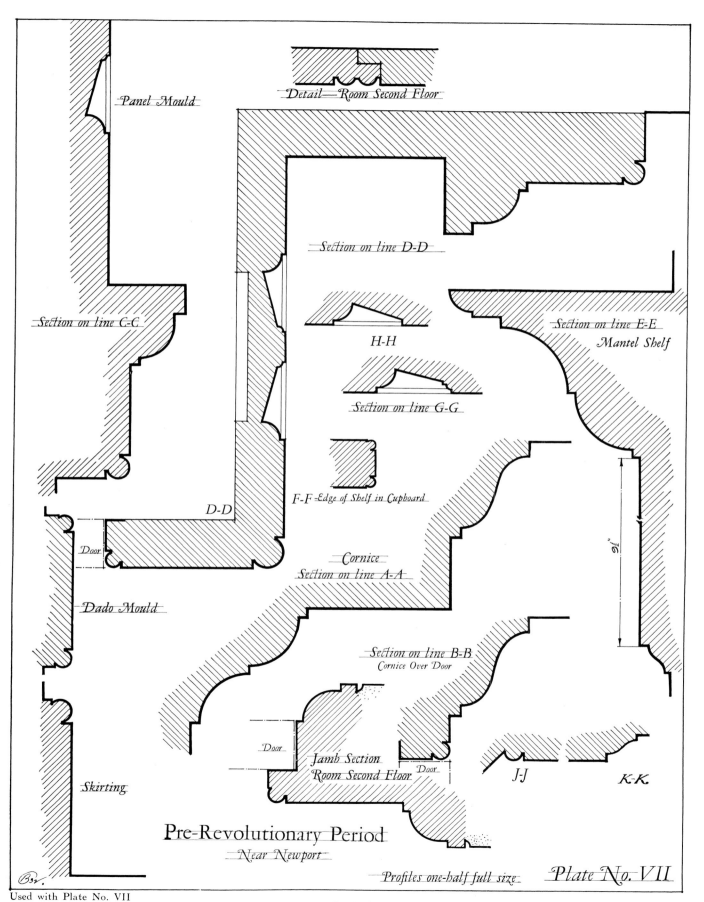

Panel Mould

Detail—Room Second Floor

Section on line D-D

H-H

Section on line C-C

Section on line G-G

Section on line E-E
Mantel Shelf

F-F—Edge of Shelf in Cupboard

D-D

Door

Cornice
Section on line A-A

Dado Mould

Section on line B-B
Cornice Over Door

Door

Jamb Section
Room Second Floor

Door

J-J

K-K

Skirting

Pre-Revolutionary Period
Near Newport

Profiles one-half full size

Plate No. VII

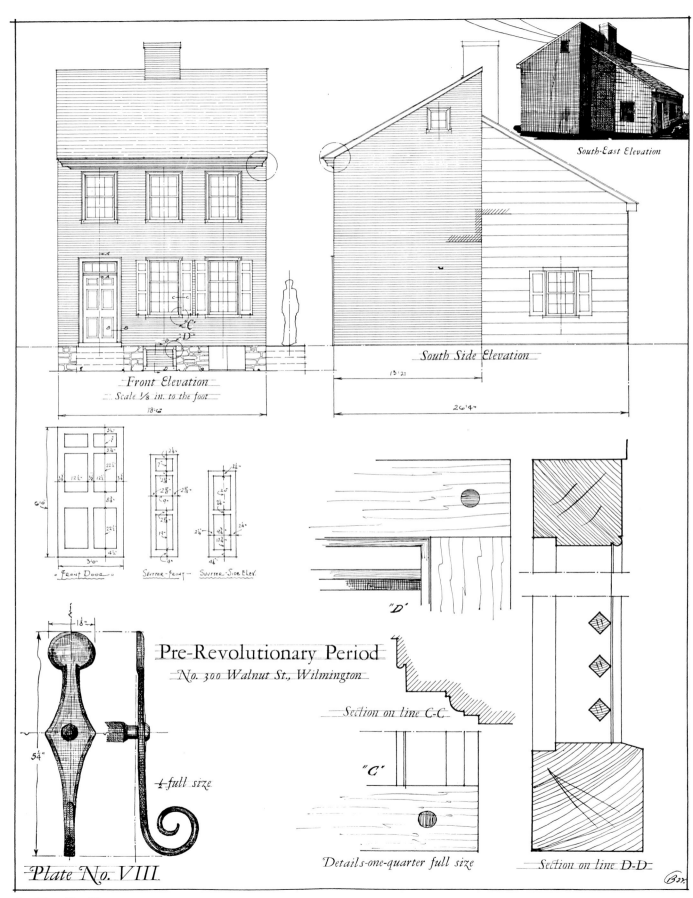

South-East Elevation

Front Elevation
Scale 1/8 in. to the foot

South Side Elevation

Front Door   Shutter-Front   Shutter-Side Elev.

"D"

Pre-Revolutionary Period
No. 300 Walnut St., Wilmington

Section on line C-C

"C"

full size

Details-one-quarter full size

Section on line D-D

Plate No. VIII

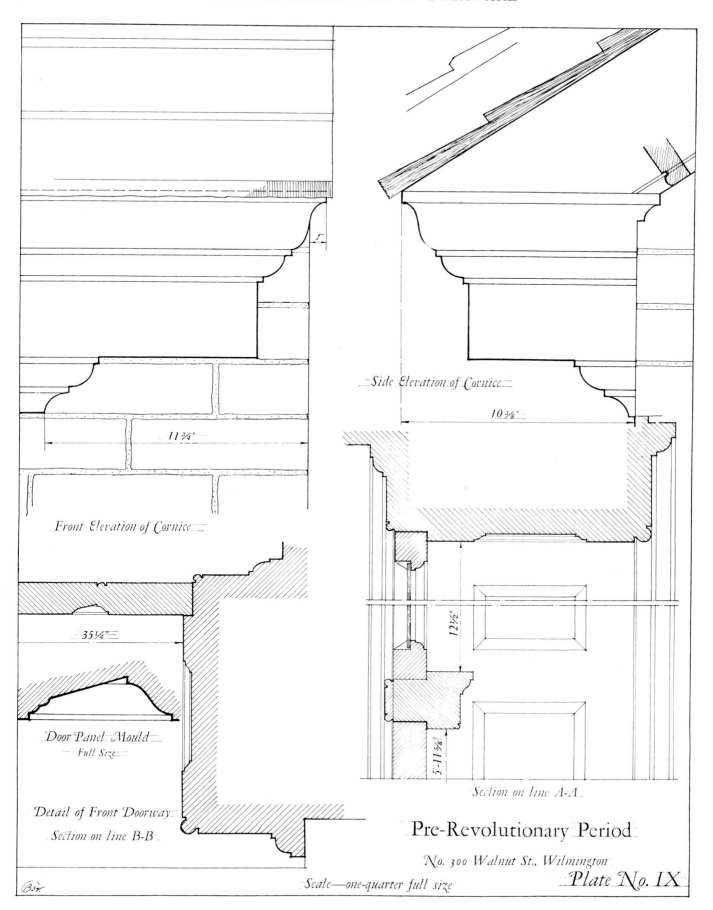

1″

Side Elevation of Cornice

10 ⅜″

Front Elevation of Cornice

11 ¾″

35 ¼″

12 ½″

Door Panel Mould
Full Size

5-11 ⅝″

Detail of Front Doorway

Section on line A-A

Section on line B-B

Pre-Revolutionary Period

No. 300 Walnut St., Wilmington

Scale—one-quarter full size

Plate No. IX

A CONJECTURAL RESTORATION SHOWING THE POSSIBILITIES OF ADAPTING DETAILS OF THE PRE-REVOLUTIONARY PERIOD TO MEET PRESENT DAY NEEDS AND TASTE

"A" Shown in illustration as the garage, Gambrel roof, Dormers, and brick (laid Flemish bond with glazed headers) may be found in both New Castle and Kent Counties.

"B" This wing is characteristic of many small houses in Kent County. The simple door with transom and blinds, is common in old work in all three counties. The walls were brick in plain pattern, and very often plastered over with smooth textures, usually natural lime in color or light buff.

"C" The Wilson and Corbit Houses in Odessa inspired this detail, although it may be found in one form or another in both New Castle and Kent Counties. Very rarely did the early settlers of Sussex County build of brick. This is especially true for the rural section, where most houses, both simple and pretentious were built of frame with shingled side walls.

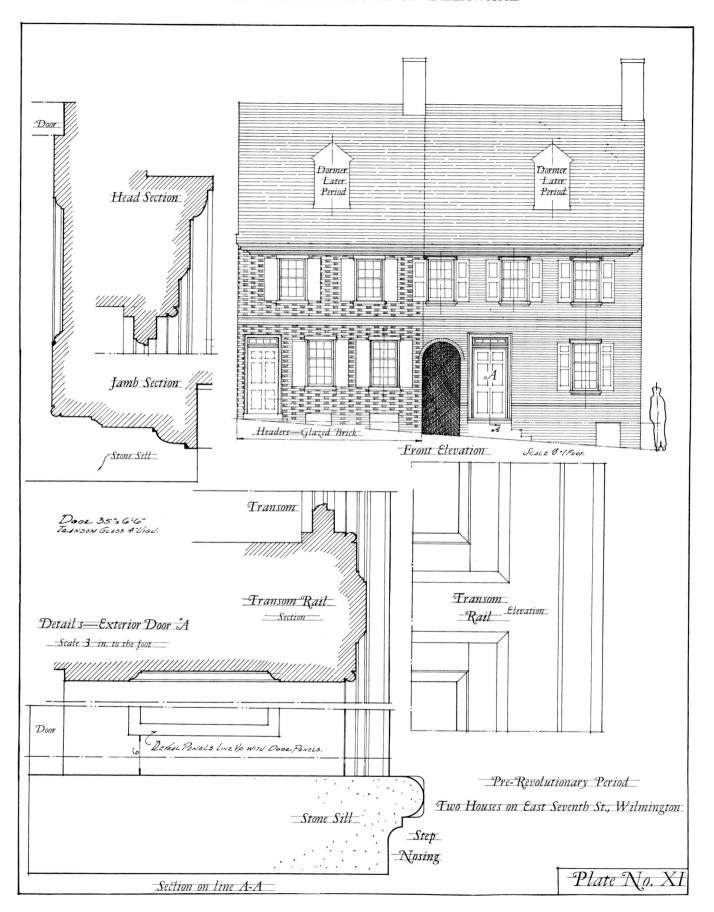

Door

Head Section

Jamb Section

Stone Sill

Dormer. Later Period.

Dormer. Later Period.

A

A

Headers—Glazed Brick

Front Elevation

Scale ⅛·1 Foot.

Door 35″x 6′6″
Transom Glass 4″ High.

Transom

Transom Rail
Section

Details—Exterior Door "A

Scale 3 in. to the foot

Door

Detail Panels Line Up with Door Panels.

Transom Rail Elevation

Stone Sill

Step

Nosing

Pre-Revolutionary Period

Two Houses on East Seventh St., Wilmington

Section on line A-A

Plate No. XI

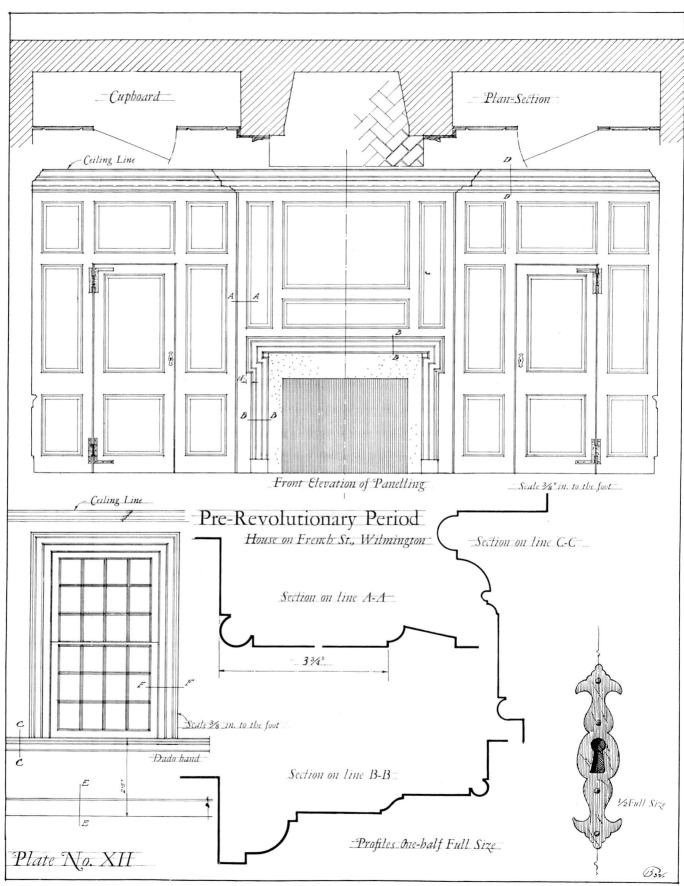

Cupboard

Plan-Section

Ceiling Line

D

A   A

B

B

B   B

Front Elevation of Panelling

Scale ⅜ in. to the foot

Ceiling Line

Pre-Revolutionary Period
House on French St., Wilmington

Section on line C-C

Section on line A-A

3¾"

F   F

C

C

Scale ⅜ in. to the foot

Dado band

E

2'5"

E

Section on line B-B

Profiles One-half Full Size

½ Full Size

Plate No. XII

See Plate No. XIII

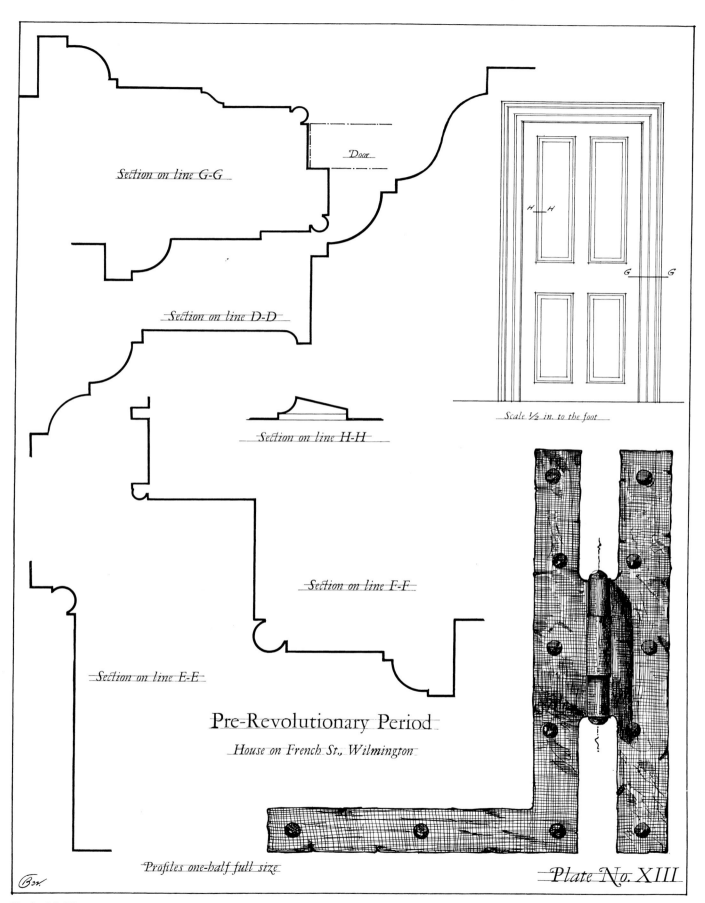

Section on line G-G

Door

Section on line D-D

Section on line H-H

Section on line F-F

Section on line E-E

Scale ½ in. to the foot

Pre-Revolutionary Period

House on French St., Wilmington

Profiles one-half full size

Plate No. XIII

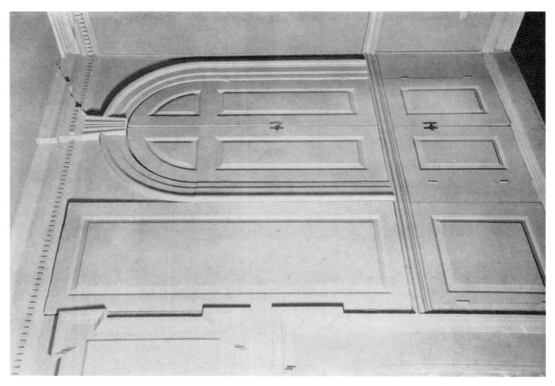

Detail in Living Room

Detail Main Facade

NICHOLAS VAN DYKE SR. HOUSE, NEW CASTLE

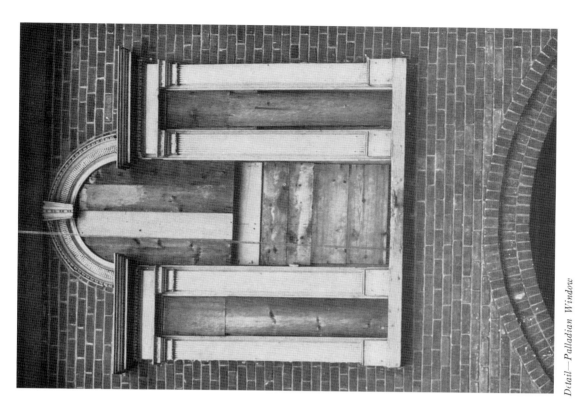

Detail—Palladian Window

OLD SCHOOL HOUSE, NEW CASTLE

Exterior View—West Entrance Door
For interior view see page 24

HOLY TRINITY (OLD SWEDES) CHURCH, WILMINGTON

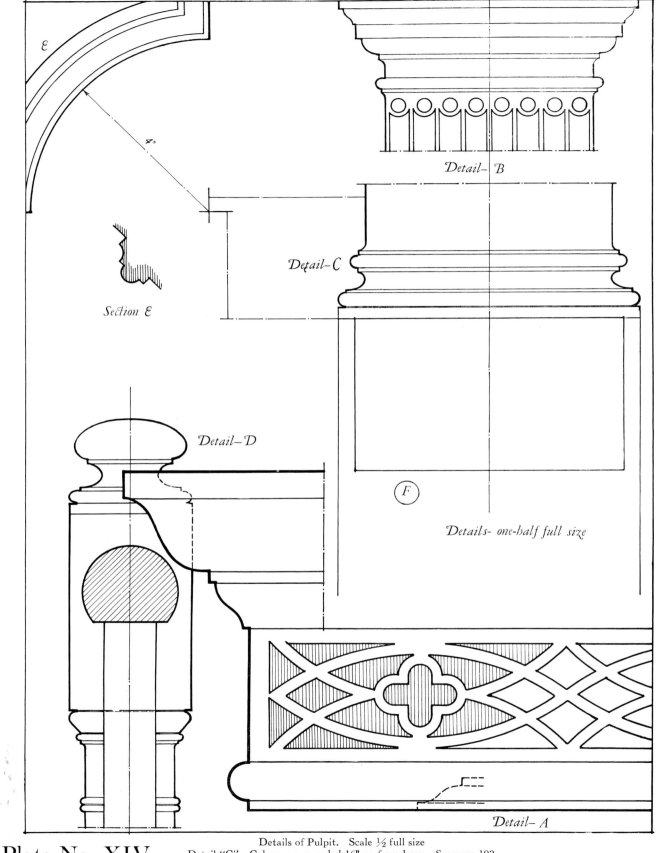

E

4"

Section E

Detail-B

Detail-C

Detail-D

F

Details- one-half full size

Detail-A

Plate No. XIV

Details of Pulpit. Scale ½ full size
Detail "C"—Columns are reeded 16" up from base. See page 192
Caps of columns "F" have same profiles as "Cap" of detail "D"

OLD DRAWYERS CHURCH, ST. GEORGES' HUNDRED

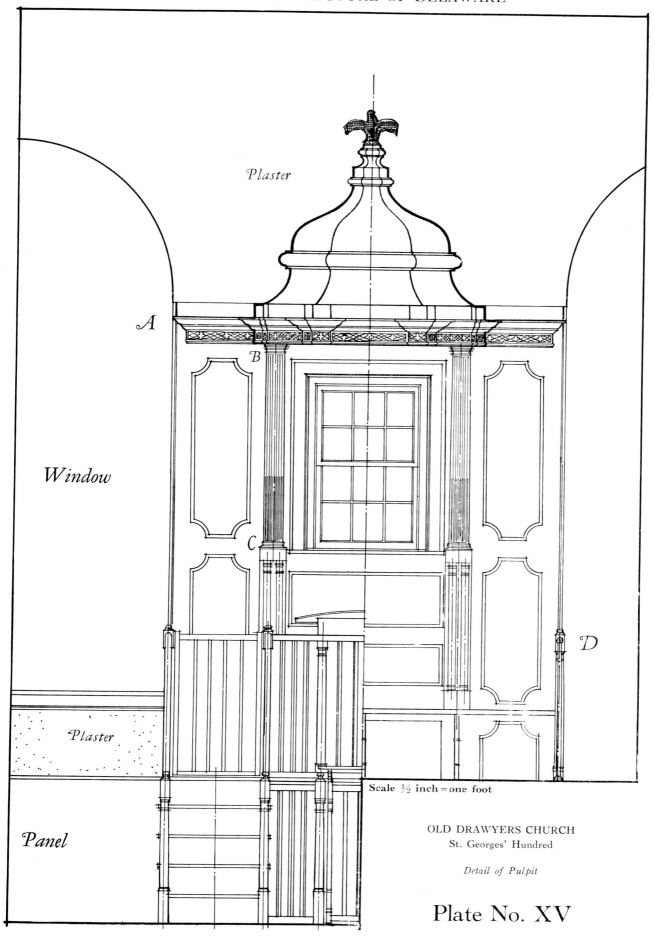

Plaster

A

B

Window

C

D

Plaster

Scale ½ inch = one foot

Panel

OLD DRAWERS CHURCH
St. Georges' Hundred

Detail of Pulpit

Plate No. XV

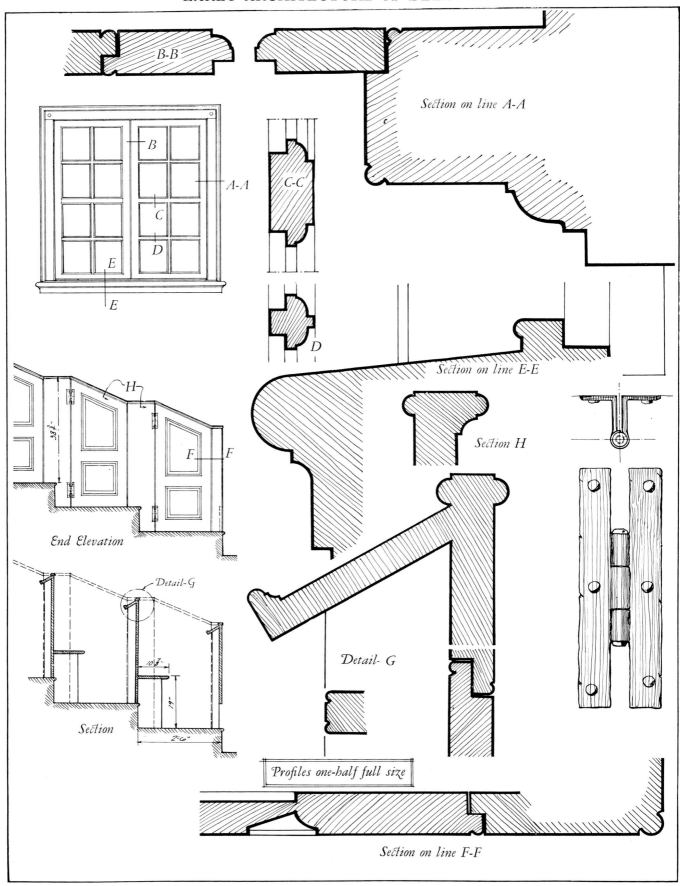

B-B

Section on line A-A

B

A-A

C-C

C

D

D

E

E

E

Section on line E-E

Section H

H

End Elevation

F F

F

Detail-G

Detail- G

Section

10¾"

19"

2'6"

Profiles one-half full size

Section on line F-F

Details—Gallery Pews and Casement Window

Plate No. XVI   HOLY TRINITY (OLD SWEDES CHURCH) WILMINGTON

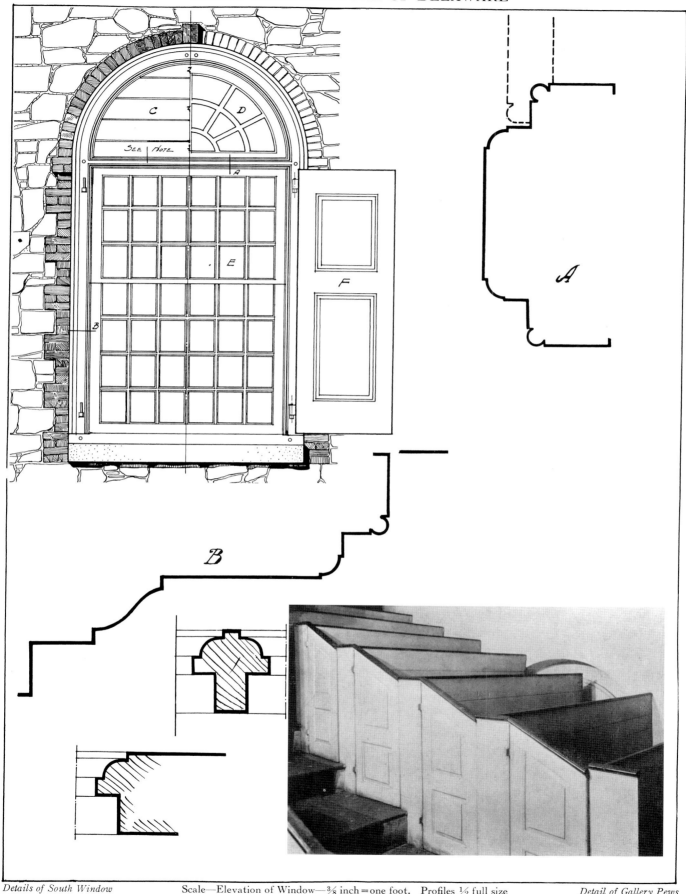

Details of South Window

Scale—Elevation of Window—⅜ inch = one foot.   Profiles ½ full size

Detail of Gallery Pews

"A" Restored—markings and return moulds indicate this profile
"C" and "D" Restored from old photographs

"E" Top sash original, lower sash restored
"F" Shutter restored from old photograph

Plate No. XVII

HOLY TRINITY (OLD SWEDES) CHURCH WILMINGTON

[181]

South Elevation
See Frontispiece, page 4

HOLY TRINITY (OLD SWEDES) CHURCH, WILMINGTON

Entrance Door
See page 54

FRIENDS' MEETING HOUSE, ODESSA

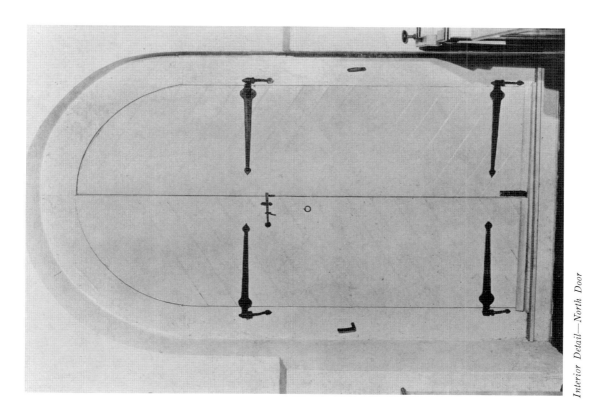

Interior Detail—North Door

HOLY TRININY (OLD SWEDES) CHURCH, WILMINGTON

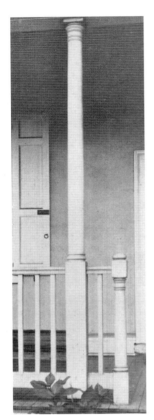

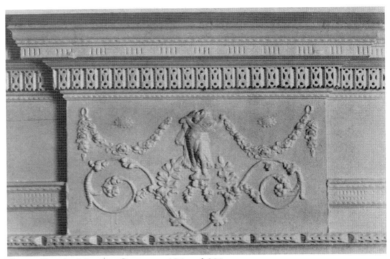

Center Panel—Mantel. See pages 104 and 105

THE VAN DYKE HOUSE
400 Delaware St., New Castle

Detail—Porch
See pages 78 and 79.

HENRY LATIMER HOUSE
Near Newport

North Entrance. See page 35
ST. JAMES' CHURCH, near Stanton

Detail—Living Room. See page 82
THE WILSON HOUSE, Odessa

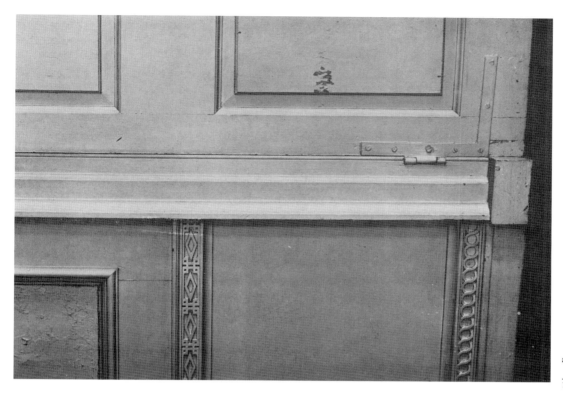

Details of Doorway—Reception Room

CORBIT HOUSE, ODESSA

See page 91

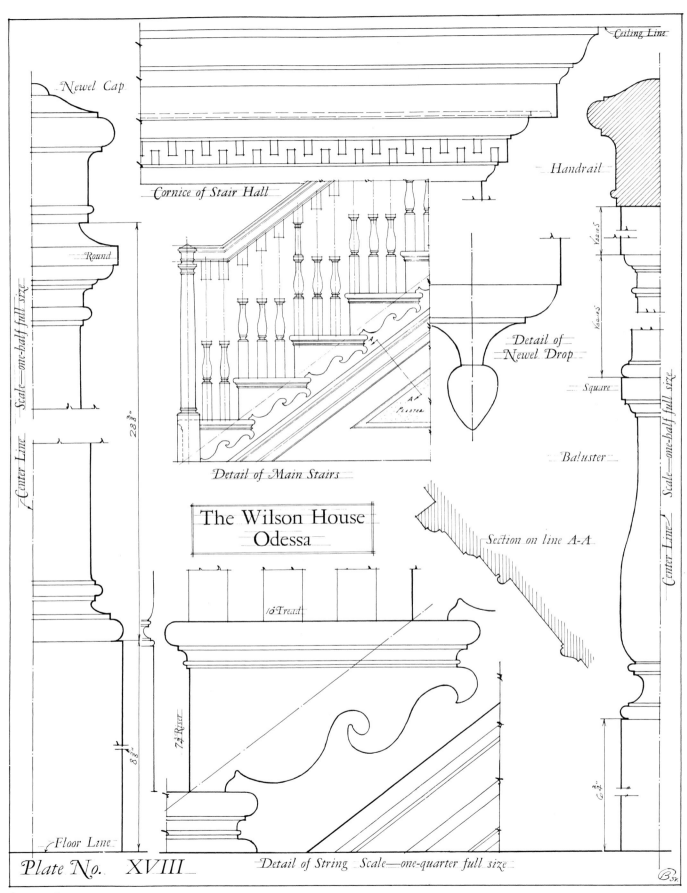

Ceiling Line

Newel Cap

Cornice of Stair Hall

Round

Handrail

Center Line   Scale—one-half full size

28⅜"

Detail of Main Stairs

Detail of Newel Drop

Baluster

The Wilson House
Odessa

Section on line A-A

16"Tread

7¼"Riser

Center Line   Scale—one-half full size

8 3/8"

6 3/4"

Floor Line

Detail of String   Scale—one-quarter full size

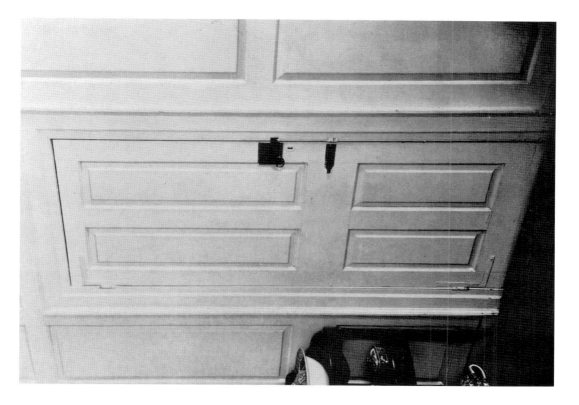

WILSON HOUSE, ODESSA

CORBIT HOUSE, ODESSA

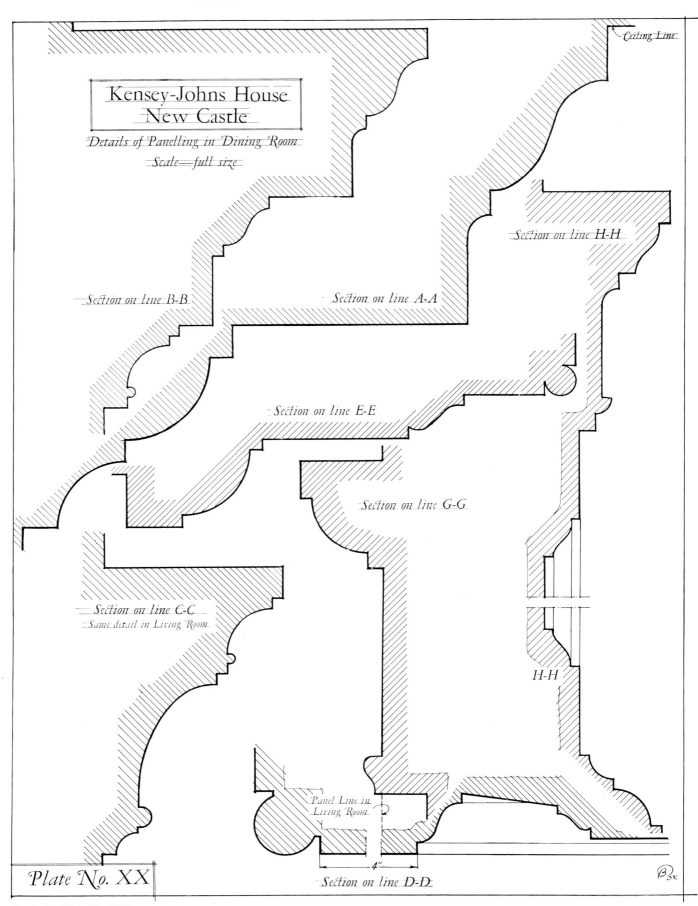

Ceiling Line

Kensey-Johns House
New Castle

Details of Panelling in Dining Room
Scale—full size

Section on line H-H

Section on line B-B

Section on line A-A

Section on line E-E

Section on line G-G

Section on line C-C
Same detail in Living Room

H-H

Panel Line in
Living Room

4"

Plate No. XX

Section on line D-D

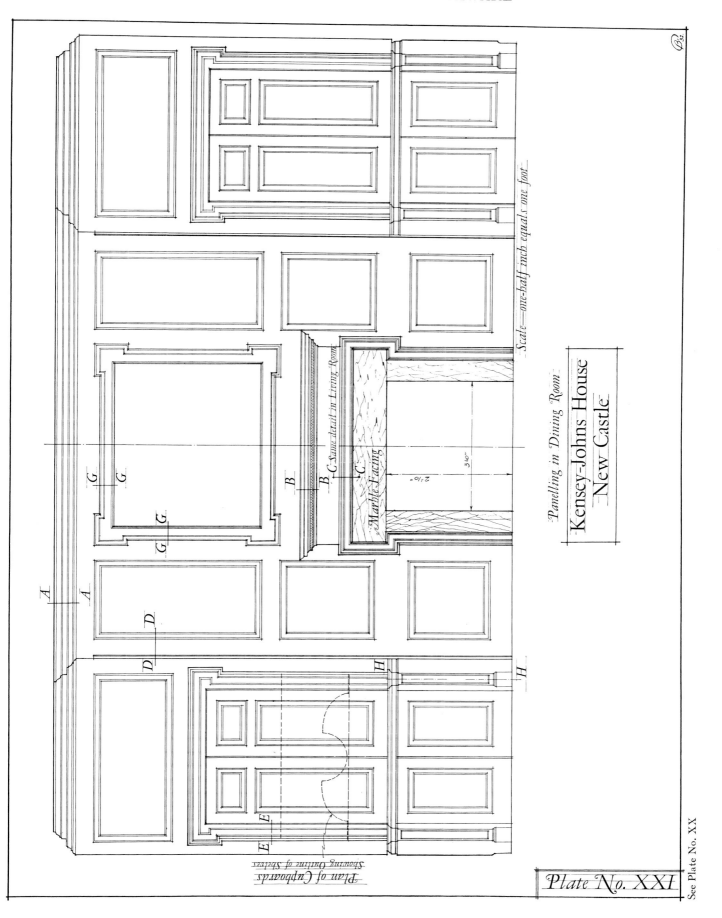

Panelling in Dining Room

**Kensey-Johns House
New Castle**

Scale—one-half inch equals one foot

*Plan of Cupboards
Showing Outline of Shelves*

Plate No. XXI

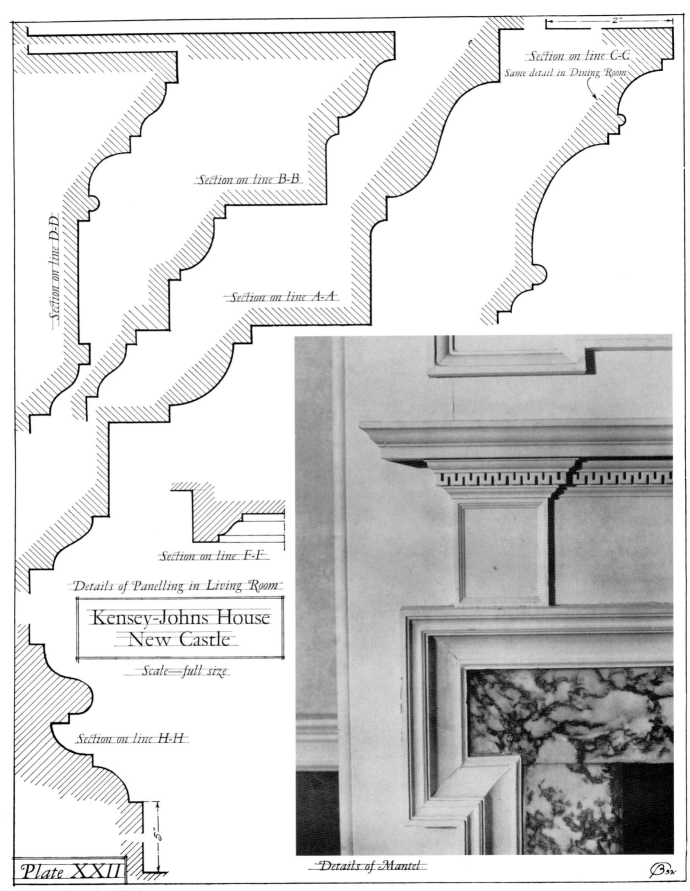

Section on line C-C

Same detail in Dining Room

Section on line B-B

Section on line D-D

Section on line A-A

Section on line F-F

Details of Panelling in Living Room

Kensey-Johns House
New Castle

Scale—full size

Section on line H-H

Details of Mantel

Plate XXII

Used with Plate No. XXIII

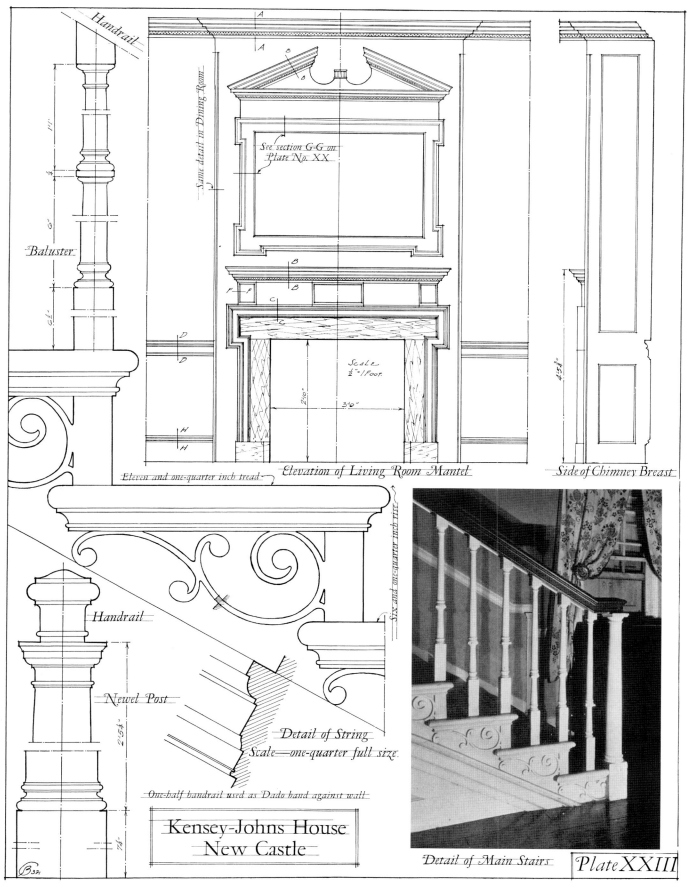

Handrail

Baluster

Same detail in Dining Room

See section G-G on Plate No. XX

Scale ½"=1 Foot.

Eleven and one-quarter inch tread

Elevation of Living Room Mantel

Side of Chimney Breast

Handrail

Newel Post

Six and one-quarter inch rise

Detail of String
Scale—one-quarter full size.

One-half handrail used as Dado band against wall

Kensey-Johns House
New Castle

Detail of Main Stairs

Plate XXIII

See Plate No. XXII

Wood Muntins

Section on line A-A

B-B

Plaster

2"

A

A

B-3

2'·11⅝"   7'·6"   2'·11⅝"

SCALE ⅜" = 1 FOOT

B   B

6'·6⅛"

Details-one-quarter full size

George Read II House
New Castle

Doorway between Reception
and Living Rooms

Section on line B-B

Center Line

Plate No. XXIV   Floor Line

See pages 120, 122, 123 and 124

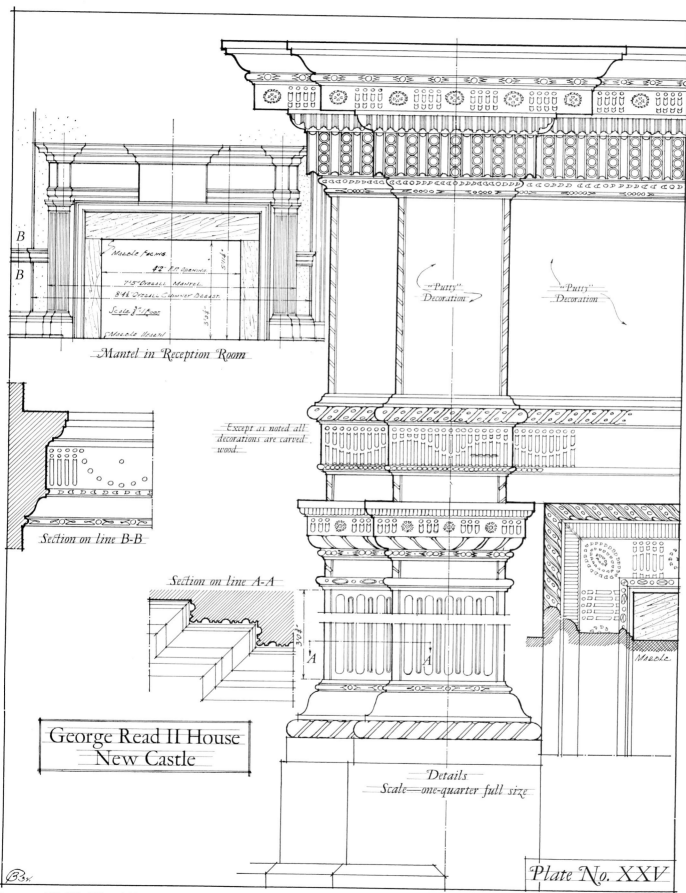

Mantel in Reception Room

Section on line B-B

Section on line A-A

"Putty" Decoration

"Putty" Decoration

Except as noted all decorations are carved wood.

Marble

George Read II House
New Castle

Details
Scale—one-quarter full size

Plate No. XXV

See pages 120, 121, 122 and 195

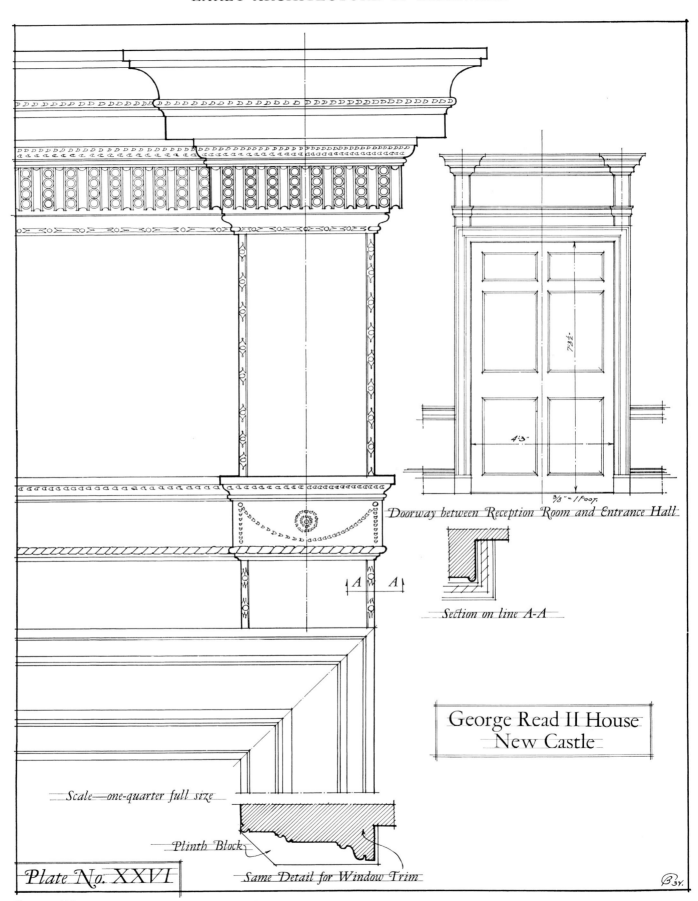

Doorway between Reception Room and Entrance Hall

3/8" = 1 Foot.

Section on line A-A

A   A

Scale—one-quarter full size

George Read II House
New Castle

Plinth Block

Same Detail for Window Trim

Center panel—Mantel in Reception Room
See page 193

Center panel—Mantel in Living Room
See page 124

GEORGE READ II HOUSE
New Castle

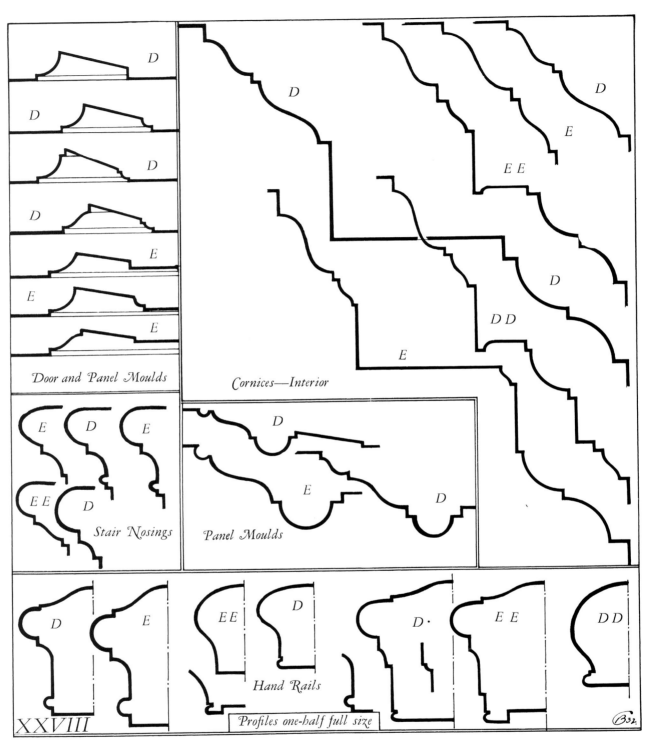

Door and Panel Moulds

Cornices—Interior

Stair Nosings

Panel Moulds

Hand Rails

XXVIII

Profiles one-half full size

"E" = Wren and Early Georgian Periods in England

"E-E" = Georgian Period in England

"D" = Pre-Revolutionary Period in Delaware

"D-D" = 1775 to 1800 Period in Delaware

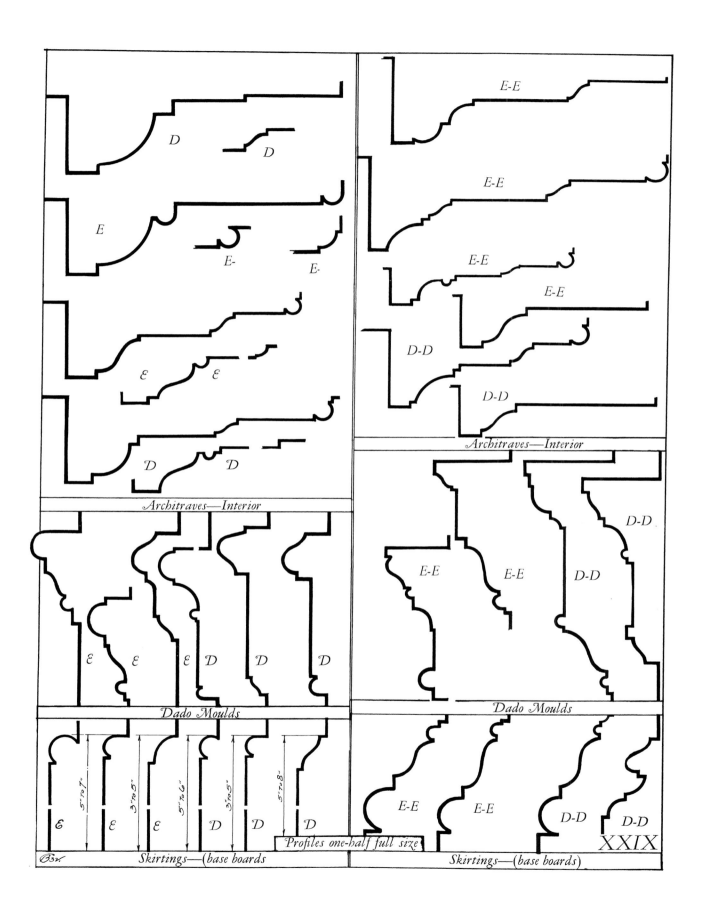

Architraves—Interior

Architraves—Interior

Dado Moulds

Dado Moulds

Profiles one-half full size

Skirtings—(base boards)

Skirtings—(base boards)

XXIX

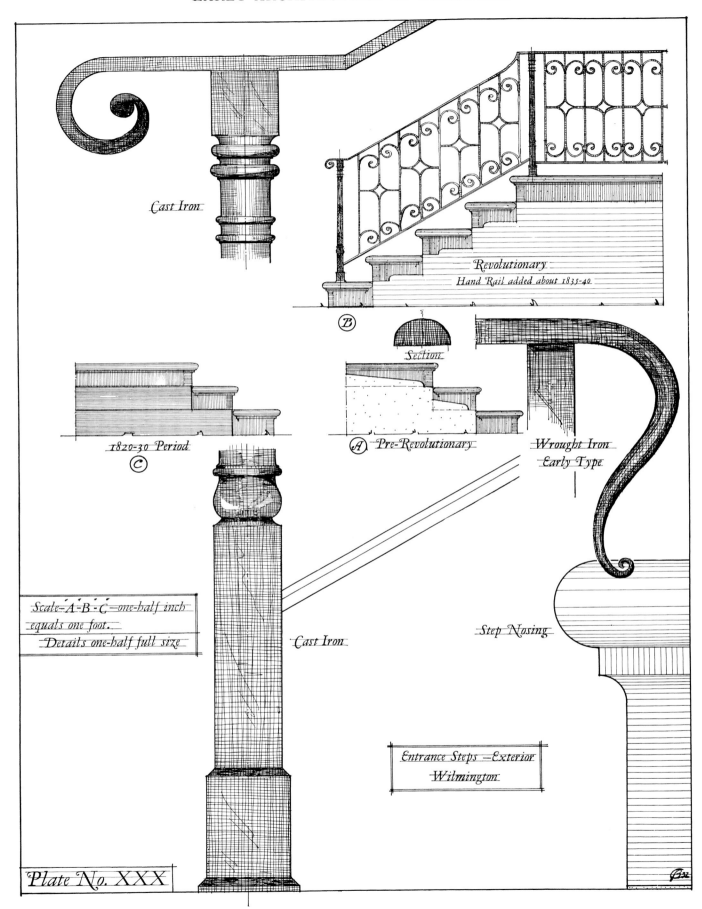

Cast Iron

Revolutionary
Hand Rail added about 1835-40

B

Section

1820-30 Period

C

A Pre-Revolutionary

Wrought Iron
Early Type

Scale—A—B—C=one-half inch
equals one foot.
Details one-half full size

Cast Iron

Step Nosing

Entrance Steps —Exterior
Wilmington

Plate No. XXX

Kensey-Johns House, New Castle
See page 95

Red Lion

Old Drawyers Church
See page 29

Christiana
See page 77

DETAILS—SMALL HOUSES

DOOR BLINDS—ODESSA

3'-1"

Ceiling Line

Window Trim

E
E
D
D

Section E-E

Dado

8'-6"

Full Size

Muntin

D-D

Full Size

Section on line A-A

Section on line B-B

2'-6"

A — A

B — B

Front Elevation of Cupboard
Scale ¾ in. to the foot

Revolutionary Period

No. 1905 Market St., Wilmington

Details one-half full size

C — C

Base 3"

Section on line C-C

Door Trim

Door between Living Room
and Entrance Hall

Scale ¾ in. to the foot

Floor Line

No. XXXVII

Red Lion

Near Centerville

Henry Clay

Terrace-Limestone Road near Corner Ketch

DETAILS—SMALL HOUSES

Price's Corner

Little Creek

Near New Castle

Yorklyn

DETAILS—SMALL HOUSES

Typical "Wishbone" Catch

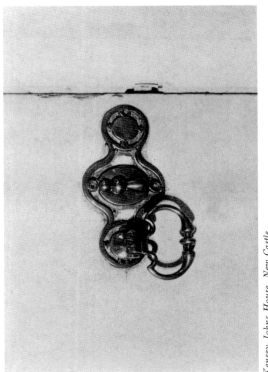

Kensey-Johns House, New Castle

Early Type Spring Latch

Woodburne, Dover

HARDWARE

Christ Church, Broad Creek

Old Swedes Church

George Read II House, New Castle

Wilmington

HARDWARE

Tavern Sign, Red Lion

INDEX

INDEX—*Continued*

INDEX—*Continued*